SAINT AUGUSTINE
AGAINST THE
ACADEMICIANS

MEDIAEVAL PHILOSOPHICAL TEXTS IN TRANSLATION

NO. 2

Marquette University Press
1131 W. Wisconsin Avenue
Milwaukee, Wisconsin

SAINT AUGUSTINE

AGAINST THE
ACADEMICIANS

(CONTRA ACADEMICOS)

Translation from the Latin
with an introduction,

By

Sister Mary Patricia Garvey, R.S.M., Ph.D.

of the Province of Detroit

MARQUETTE UNIVERSITY PRESS   MILWAUKEE, WISCONSIN   1957

Nihil Obstat

H. B. Ries
Censor Librorum
St. Francis, Wis., Die 1 Septembris, 1942

Imprimatur

✝Moyses E. Kiley
Milwaukiae, Die 4 Septembris, 1942
Archiepiscopus Milwaukiensis

ST. AUGUSTINE *AGAINST THE ACADEMICIANS*

INTRODUCTION

I. Life of St. Augustine

AURELIUS AUGUSTINE was born at Tagaste in Numidia, on November 13, 354 A.D. His father, Patricius, was a pagan, who received the grace of baptism shortly before his death; his mother, the saintly Monica, who enrolled the infant Augustine among the catechumens and imbued his early years with Christian impressions which never completely vanished from his soul.

Augustine rceived his education at Tagaste and then at Madaura. Later on Patricius, realizing the splendid educational advantages afforded by the schools of Carthage, sent his brilliant son to complete his education in the cultured but vicious metropolis of northern Africa. Here, while pursuing his liberal studies with eminent success, he was lured by evil companions into the life of carnal indulgence which he so graphically describes in the *Confessions.*

In his nineteenth year after having read Cicero's exhortation to philosophy, Augustine hastened to the Scriptures in search of the wisdom which the *Hortensius* urged him to pursue; for wisdom, he believed, must be associated with the name of Christ. Disappointed, however, with the simplicity of their style, he joined the Manichaeans in search of the knowledge for which he longed. Meanwhile, after having completed his studies, he became a professor of rhetoric at Carthage and later at Rome.

After nine years of adherence to the Manichaeans, Augustine, impressed by the many inconsistencies of their doctrines, abandoned their tenets. Overwhelmed by disappointment, he despaired of ever finding the truth, and turned to the New Academy whose basic principle was that probability in the realm of knowledge is all that man can hope to attain. At this juncture the young professor changed his residence from Rome to Milan where he became interested in the writings of the Neo-Platonists and where he fortunately came under the influence of St. Ambrose, the bishop of Milan. Gradually Augustine's doubts subsided and, moved by the grace of God, he was converted to the Catholic faith. To the delight of his pious mother who for years had poured forth prayers and tears that God would enlighten the darkness of her son, Augustine was baptized by St. Ambrose at Easter in 387 A.D.

The following year Augustine returned to Africa. In 391 A.D. he was ordained a priest and in 395 was made the bishop of Hippo. From the time

[1]

of his conversion until his death in 430 A.D. he unceasingly combated heresies, particularly Manichaeism, Donatism, and Pelagianism, and devoted whatever time he could spare from his ecclesiastical duties, to literary pursuits.

II. Philosophical Works

To determine with precision the philosophical writings of Saint Augustine involves a problem of no little difficulty. So intimately are philosophy and theology united in his works that it is somewhat perplexing to decide what treatises rightly should be listed as philosophic studies.

It would seem that the treatises written by Augustine shortly before his baptism and several of those composed within a few years after this important event are chiefly concerned with truths not beyond the reach and power of reason. Hence, these studies may properly be regarded as Augustine's philosophic works. They include:

1. *Contra Academicos*, written at Cassiciacum in 386 A.D. It aims to prove that man can attain certitude and therefore need not be content with mere probability in the realm of knowledge.
2. *De beata vita*, composed in 386 A.D. at Cassiciacum. It is devoted to the subject of happiness. The conclusion is that true happiness can be found only in the knowledge of God.
3. *De ordine*, likewise written at Cassiciacum before Augustine's baptism. It investigates the rôle of evil in the designs of Providence.
4. *Soliloquia*, the last of the dialogues composed at Cassiciacum. It establishes the immortality of the human soul.
5. *De immortalitate animae*, a sequel to the *Soliloquia*, written at Milan in 387 A.D. It proves the immortality of the soul by the ability of the human mind to recognize truth.
6. *De quantitate animae*, composed at Rome in 388 A.D. It is a study of the dignity and grandeur of the human soul.
7. *De libero arbitrio*, begun at Rome during the winter of 387-388 A.D. and completed after Augustine's return to Africa. It discusses the origin and nature of moral evil.
8. *De musica*, commenced before Augustine's baptism at Milan and concluded in Africa about 389 A.D. The first five books treat of the technique of rhythm, metre, and verse. The sixth book passes from the consideration of sensible numbers to those which have no relation to that which is corporeal, but are unchangeable and found in immutable truth.
9. *De magistro*, written in Africa in 389 A.D. It presents Augustine's theory of knowledge and develops his celebrated doctrine of the Word, as the interior Master of the human intellect.

Of Augustine's later writings the *De anima et eius origine*, a treatise on the origin and nature of the human soul, may well be ranked among his philosophical works. The *Confessionum libri XIII*, his celebrated autobiography, discusses many problems of philosophical interest, though they are not from a philosophical point of view. The same may be said of the *De*

[2]

Trinitate. The *De civitate Dei*, Augustine's monumental work, which has been called the first philosophy of history, and the *Retractationes*, in which Augustine makes a revision of his works, likewise deserve a place among the treatises which have a philosophical interest.

III. *Contra Academicos*

A. Historical Treatment of the Treatise

Our sources for determining the date of composition of the works of St. Augustine are the *Retractationes* and internal evidence in the writings themselves. In the prologue of the *Retractationes* Augustine observes: 'Whoever reads my little works in the order in which they were written will perhaps learn how I progressed in writing them. In order that he may be able to do this, I shall take pains, in so far as I can, in this little work, that he may know the same order.'

The *Contra Academicos* is the first work mentioned in the *Retractationes*; hence it would seem to have been the first commenced by Augustine.[1] However, he tells us that the three books comprising the treatise were not written consecutively. The *De beata vita*, he observes, was not composed 'after the books concerning the Academicians, but between them,'[2] and the *De ordine* was produced 'between those books which were written concerning the Academicians.'[3] Internal evidence in the *Contra Academicos* and *De ordine* would seem to indicate that the *De beata vita* and the first book of the *De ordine* were written between the first and second books of the *Contra Academicos*.[4] According to a chart prepared by D. Ohlmann[5] on data obtained from internal evidence in the early works of Augustine, the discussions contained in the three books of the *Contra Academicos* were held on November 10, 11, 20, 21 and 22, in 386 A.D.

From Augustine himself[6] we learn the reason for his having devoted his first literary efforts to a refutation of skepticism. Shortly after he had resigned his profession, thereby severing his relations with the world, he tells us, he directed his attention to the problem of certitude which is of vital importance in establishing a foundation for knowledge. In order permanently to eliminate any influence which the doctrine of uncertainty professed by the Academicians might have exerted upon him, he wished completely to break down the arguments which they alleged in support of the

---

[1] *Retractationes*, I, i, 1.
[2] *Ibid.*, I, ii, 1.
[3] *Ibid.*, I, iii, 1.
[4] Cf. *Contra Academicos*, I, ii, 5; I, iii, 8; II, iv, 10; II, viii, 20; III, i, 1; *De ordine*, I, iii, 7.
[5] Cf. D. Ohlmann, *De sancti Augustini dialogis in Cassiciaco scriptis* (Strasbourg: "Der Elsasser" Printing Press, 1897), p. 27.
[6] *Retractationes*, I, i, 1.

impossibility of finding the truth, and the expediency of refusing to give assent to anything.

The source from which Augustine probably derived his information concerning the doctrine of the Academicians was Cicero's *Academica*. Augustine's profound respect for the great Roman genius and admiration for his scholarship, as well as internal evidence in the *Contra Academicos* itself, would lead us to arrive at this conclusion. In the course of the discussions Cicero is mentioned several times by Augustine and his pupils.[7] Augustine speaks of him as a defender of the doctrine of the Academicians[8] and quotes directly from the *Academica* as well as from other works of the Roman philosopher. Also similarities in terminology and by way of illustration are not infrequently to be noted in the *Academica* of Cicero and Augustine's *Contra Academicos*.[9]

B. Synopsis of *Contra Academicos*

This treatise, consisting of three books, is dedicated to Romanianus, the generous benefactor who in Augustine's youth had made possible the continuation of his studies and had consoled and assisted him upon the death of his father. The participants in the disputation are Augustine, his pupils: Licentius and Trygetius, and his friend Alypius.

The first book of the dialogue is concerned with the subject of truth in its relation to happiness. Is it possible for a man to be happy if he has not attained the knowledge of truth? In order to answer this question it seems necessary to define happiness. Augustine suggests that happiness consists in living in accordance with that which is best in man, namely, his reason. On the basis of this definition Licentius affirms that the search for truth without the possession of it is sufficient to render one happy. Trygetius objects to this assertion on the ground that one who is in error can not be said to live in accordance with reason. Now, he is in error who seeks but does not find truth; hence, such a man is not happy.

It seems advisable at this point to consider the meaning of error. Trygetius is of the opinion that to err consists always in seeking but never finding. Licentius defines it as the giving of one's assent to that which is false. But, he adds, one who is searching for truth lives in accordance with reason and does not assent to what is false. Such a man, inasmuch as he lives in harmony with reason, is happy. Therefore one can attain happiness merely by seeking truth, even though he can by no means find it.

---

[7] Cf. *Contra Academicos,* I, i, 4; I, iii, 7; I, iii, 8; I, ix, 25; II, i, 1; III, vii, 15; III, viii, 17; III, xx, 43; III, xx, 45.

[8] Cf. *Ibid.,* III, vii, 15.

[9] These similarities will be pointed out in the notes which accompany this translation of the *Contra Academicos*.

[4]

The question next arises as to whether the man who is earnest in his quest for truth, possesses wisdom. Is not the wise man rather he who has found and is enjoying truth? In order to answer these questions it seems advisable to define wisdom. Since his pupils can not agree upon a definition, Augustine proposes that recommended by the Ancients: wisdom is the knowledge of things human and divine. Licentius takes exception to this definition and after considerable argument with Trygetius, expresses the opinion that human wisdom is the search for truth, which results in a happy life on account of the peace of mind which it affords. At this point Augustine, after reviewing the argument as developed by his pupils, discontinues the discussion by bidding Licentius, who seems to favor the Academicians on the subject of truth, to prepare stronger arguments to defend them, since it is his intention to make charges against the Academicians.

After seven days elapsed, Augustine and his friends resume their argument on the Academicians, the discussion comprising the second book of the *Contra Academicos*.

At the request of Licentius, Augustine gives a summary of the doctrine of the Academicians. They held, he says, that man can not attain certitude in regard to philosophic truths. It is the duty of a wise man, therefore, merely to seek truth. He should never assent to anything, for by so doing he assents to what is uncertain and therefore falls into error. In order to prove conclusively that truth can not be found, the Academicians emphasized the basic doctrine of Zeno, the Stoic, namely, that truth can be grasped only by signs such as that which is false can not have. But although suspension of assent is the great achievement of the wise man, for all practical purposes he can hold to a kind of probability which, as they said, bears a similarity to truth.

At the suggestion of Augustine, Alypius explains the difference between the doctrine of the Old and the New Academy. Although Socrates, Plato, and the older Academicians advised that one should not rashly give assent, they did not make any special inquiry as to whether or not truth can be known. It was Zeno who held that nothing can be known unless it is so true as to be distinguished from the false by differentiating notes, and that a conjecture ought never to enter the mind of a wise man. Arcesilaus, proceeding further, maintained that nothing certain can be known and that one should not give assent to anything. Finally, Antiochus, a pupil of Philo, attempted to show that the doctrine of the New Academy was far removed from that of the Old. However, he defended nothing more than that the wise man is able to comprehend truth.

Alypius then offers to support the doctrine of the Academicians, since it is his personal opinion and also the teaching of eminent philosophers

[5]

whose authority ought to have weight, that truth has not yet been found. Augustine holds the opposite view and announces as the subject of the next disputation to be held between Alypius and himself the possibility of arriving at truth.

In the third book of the *Contra Academicos* Augustine devotes himself wholeheartedly to the refutation of the Academicians. Reason assures us, he observes, that the wise man knows wisdom. Now, the Academicians are of the opinion that man can be wise and yet that he can not attain certain knowledge. But, as has been said, reason demands that the wise man knows wisdom, which certainly does not mean that he knows nothing. Therefore, one must grant either that wisdom is nothing or that the wise man is portrayed by the Academicians as a person of whom reason will not admit. Since, then, the Academicians at one and the same time maintained that man can be wise and yet possess no certain knowledge, it is necessary to reject their doctrine. In knowing wisdom, therefore, one knows something. But it is universally agreed—even the Academicians admitted this—that one can not know error. Hence, in knowing wisdom one must know truth.

Alypius acknowledges this error on the part of the Academicians, but he still holds that their argument in regard to the suspension of assent has not been invalidated. Augustine then proceeds completely to weaken the position of the Academicians. They based their doctrine that truth can not be known on the definition of Zeno, but that very definition renders it easy to refute them. For Zeno said that whatever has no mark in common with that which is false can be grasped as true. Now, if that definition is true, he who knows it, knows something true; if it is false, it should in no way influence man. And if one merely holds that it is either true or false, by that very disjunction he admits that he knows something true. Even a person who makes no pretense of being wise has certitude about some things, for example, that there is one world or more than one; that these worlds are finite or infinite in number. Such propositions are indisputably true.

But, Carneades would say, how do you even know that there is a world, since the senses are so unreliable? It is true, Augustine observes, that by means of the senses we know only the appearance of reality. But in the performance of this function they are indeed trustworthy and provide us with certain knowledge. However, it is reason, the highest power in man, which judges, so that whatever he is unable to acquire by means of the senses is granted to him by the avenue of reason. So the wise man has no ground for withholding his assent, for, since the wise man knows wisdom itself, as has already been granted, it would be even more unheard of for him not to assent to wisdom than it would be not to know wisdom.

[6]

Moreover, the Academicians, Augustine says, were not in reality skeptics. In all probability they were the disciples of Plato and were merely concealing their true sentiments from those who, steeped in materialism as Zeno was, could not appreciate the sublime doctrines of the founder of the Academy. For he taught that there are two worlds: an intelligible world in which truth resides, and a sensible world which is the image of the other and in which knowledge, strictly speaking, is unattainable.

Hence, Augustine concludes, it is indeed evident that man can arrive at truth. And there are two sources, he adds, from which this pearl of inestimable value can be derived, "the double weight of authority and reason."

C. Retractationes

The *Retractationes* contains a revision of his works, which Augustine made a few years before his death. In the course of his literary activities he admitted that his intellectual outlook had changed somewhat as time elapsed. 'I endeavor,' he facetiously observed, 'to be one of those who write by progressing and who progress by writing.'[10] This change of attitude toward men and doctrines is embodied in the *Retractationes*[11] in which the illustrious Bishop of Hippo takes pains to clarify doctrines expressed in certain passages of his writings lest anyone mistake their import,[12] as well as to note specific alterations in his point of view.

In order to set forth with precision Augustine's estimate of the *Contra Academicos*, expressed some forty years after the composition of the treatise, we have considered it advisable to present his criticism as he himself proposes it.

When I had renounced the ambitions of this world, which I either had attained or desired to attain, and had devoted myself to the peace of a Christian life, though not yet baptized, I wrote first of all against the Academicians or concerning the Academicians, so that by the best reasons within my power I might banish from my mind their arguments, since they were exerting an influence upon me, which force upon many despair of finding the truth and prevent the wise man from giving assent to anything and approving of anything whatever, as if it were manifest and certain, since in their opinion everything seems to be obscure and uncertain. This was accomplished by the mercy and help of the Lord.

But I am displeased for having used so many times in the same three books the name 'fortune,' although it was my intention not that any goddess be understood by this term, but the fortuitous outcome of events, whether good or evil, in regard to our body or to extraneous matters. Whence are those words which no religion for-

---

[10] *Epistulae*, CXLIII, 2.
   Cf. *De dono perseverantiae*, II, xii; also *De praedestinatione Sanctorum*, I, iii-iv.
[11] The *Retractationes* is found in J. P. Migne, *Patrologia Latina*. XXXII, 583-656.
[12] Cf. *De dono perseverantiae*, II, xiv, 70; also *Contra Julianum*, V, v; V, ix.

bids us to use: by chance [*forte*],perhaps [*forsan*], by luck [*forsitan*], peradventure [*fortasse*], by accident [*fortuito*], which nevertheless ought wholly to be referred to Divine Providence. This point, too, I did not pass over in silence since I thereupon said: '*For perhaps what is usually called fortune is directed by a certain hidden Providence and we call it nothing else but chance when the reason for it is unknown.*'[13] I said this, it is true, but still I regret having thus used the word fortune in that passage since I see that men are addicted to the very pernicious habit of saying, 'fortune has willed this' whereas it ought to be said, 'God has willed this.' Moreover, in regard to what I said in a certain place: '*It has been so arranged either in proportion to our merits or by the necessity of nature, that the mind which is of divine origin can by no means, while clinging to perishable things, he admitted into the harbor of philosophy*'[14] and so forth, either both of these statements ought not have been made, because even then the meaning could be obvious, or it was enough to say: '*in proportion to our merits,*' as it is true that our misfortune was derived from Adam; nor was there any need of adding, '*or by the necessity of nature,*' since indeed the stern necessity of our nature had its origin in the punishment of the sin preceding it. In that part also in which I said: '*Nothing at all should be cherished and everything should be despised which mortal eye can see or any sense can appropriate,*[15] words should be added so that the statement would be: whatever a sense of the corruptible body appropriates, for there is also a sense of the mind. But I was speaking then after the manner of those who use the word 'sense' only in reference to that of the body, and 'sensible' only in regard to that which is corporeal. And so, whenever I spoke in this fashion, I made too little effort to avoid ambiguity except with those who are in the habit of speaking in this way. I likewise said: '*Do you think that to live happily is anything else than to live according to that which is best in man?*'[16] And I explained shortly afterwards what I considered to be best in man: '*Who,*' I said, '*would doubt that nothing else is best in man than that part of the soul to which it is fitting that all other things which are in man should submit as to their ruler? But lest you demand another definition, this [part] can be called the intellect or reason.*'[17] This is indeed true—for in so far as it pertains to the nature of man, there is nothing in him better than his intellect and reason—but it is not in accordance with reason itself that he ought to live who wishes to live happily. Otherwise he lives according to man, though he ought to live according to God in order that he may be able to arrive at [that] happiness for whose attainment reason of itself is not bound to be solicitous, but our intellect must be subjected to God. Also in replying to him with whom I was engaged in discussion, I said: '*In this respect you are not wholly in error because I desired very much that you should have an augury*

---

[13] *Contra Academicos,* I ,i, 1.
[14] *Ibid.,* I, i,1.
[15] *Ibid.,* I, i, 3.
[16] *Ibid.,* I, ii, 5.
[17] *Ibid.,* I, ii, 5.

[omen] for your remaining arguments.'[18] Although I did not say this in earnest, but by way of a joke, still I should be unwilling to use this word. Indeed, I do not recall having read the word *omen* in our sacred literature or in the diction of any ecclesiastical disputant, although it is derived from *abominatio* which is continuously found in the Sacred Books.[19]

In the second book is found that absolutely foolish and absurd fable, as it were, about philocalia and philosophy, that they are sisters and were begotten by the same parent. For either what is called philocalia exists merely in words and therefore is in no respect a sister of philosophy, or if it is a name deserving of honor, due to the fact that from its Latin interpretation it signifies love of beauty, and if the beauty of wisdom is real and of the highest order, philocalia in matters incorporeal and most elevated is itself the same as philosophy, nor are they in any way, as it were, two sisters. In another place when I was treating of the soul, I said:'*[It] will return more securely into heaven.'*[20] However, I should have said 'will go' rather than 'will return' more securely on account of those who think that human souls have fallen from heaven as a punishment for their sins, or after having been cast out, are forced into those bodies. But I did not hesitate on that account to use the expression, because I said 'into heaven' in such a way as I would say 'to God' Who is its [the soul's] Author and Creator, as Holy Cyprian has not hesitated to say: 'For since we have our body from the earth and our soul from heaven, we ourselves are of the earth and heaven.'[21] And in the Book of *Ecclesiastes* it is written: 'The spirit will return to God Who gave it.'[22] This certainly ought to be understood in such a way as not to be in opposition to the Apostle who says: 'When not yet born, [the children] had not done any good or evil.'[23] Therefore God Himself is indisputably a kind of original habitation of beatitude for the soul, not indeed in the sense that He produced it from His own essence, but that He formed it from no other substance as He fashioned the body from the earth. For in regard to its origin, how it happens that it is in the body, whether from that one which was first created when 'man was made into a living soul,'[24] or whether they are made similarly one by one, I did not know then nor do I know at present.[25]

---

[18] *Contra Academicos,* II, iii, 7.
[19] Augustine may have reference to *Deuteronomy* in which the word appears fourteen times.
[20] *Contra Academicos,* II, ix, 22.
[21] St. Cyprian, *De Domini oratione.*
[22] *Ecclesiastes,* XII, 7.
[23] *Romans,* IX, 11.
[24] *Genesis,* II, vii, 15; I. *Corinthians,* XV, 45.
[25] Even toward the close of his life Augustine seemed unable precisely to decide how human souls come into existence. The transmission of original sin caused him to incline somewhat to the theory of traducianism. However, he also seemed to lean toward the doctrine of creationism, according to which each human soul is created immediately at the moment of generation. Cf. *De Genesi ad litteram,* VII, iii-iv; *De anima et eius origine,* II, iii, 6; *Epistulae,* CLXIII, CLXIV, CLXVI, CXC, CXL; *De libero arbitrio,* III, LV-LIX.

In the third book I said: '*If you ask me my opinion, I think that the highest good of man lies in his intellect.*' I should more truly have said: in God; for it is in Him as its own highest good, that the intellect finds its joy in order to be happy. Nor does it please me to have said: '*I can swear by all that is divine.*'[26] Also the statement I made about the Academicians, that they knew the truth whose likeness they called the likeness of truth and that I called that very likeness of truth false, to which they assented,[27] was not correctly expressed for two reasons: either because it would be false that it in some manner would be like some truth, since in its own and this way it is true, or because they assented to those false [ideas] which they called [ideas] having the likeness of truth, though they would not assent to anything and affirmed that the wise man does not assent to anything.[28] But I happened to say this about them because they also gave the name probable to this very likeness ‘of truth. Also the very praise which I bestowed upon Plato and the Platonists or the Academician philosophers[29] in such measure as was not due to impious men, rightly displeased me, especially [the praise of those] against whose great errors Christian teaching is to be defended. That also which I said were my trivialities [*nugas*][30] in comparison with the arguments of Cicero, which he used in his *Academica*, by which I refuted those arguments by a most certain process of reasoning, even though it was said by way of jest, and seems rather a dissimulation, still I ought not have said it.

IV. Bibliography

A.   Sources on the Life of St. Augustine

Our most reliable and, consequently, most important source of information on the life of St. Augustine until shortly after his conversion, is his celebrated autobiography, the *Confessions*, written about the year 400 A.D.[31] In this work Augustine relates the history of his struggles, his hesitations, his progress both intellectual and moral, until he formally embraced Christianity and was baptized in 387 A.D. This narrative concludes with the death of his mother, St. Monica, while they were en route to Africa in 387 A.D. Isolated biographical references also occur in other writings of Augustine, chiefly in the *Epistulae*, and in the dialogues written at Cassiciacum.

---

26 *Contra Academicos*, III, xvi, 35.
27 *Ibid.*, III, xviii, 40.
28 *Ibid.*, II, vi, 14.
29 *Ibid.*, III, xvii, 37; also II, x, 24.
30 *Ibid.*, III, xx, 45.
31 The Benedictine Editors of the *Opera omnia* of Augustine assign 400 A.D. as the date of composition of the *Confessions* because this work is mentioned by Augustine in the *Retractationes* just before the treatise against Faustus, the Manichaean which was written not much before or after this year. Cf. *Patrologia Latina* XXXII, 659-660.

The most ancient biographer of St. Augustine was Possidius, bishop of Calama in Numidia, an intimate friend and contemporary of Augustine. His *Vita sancti Aurelii Augustini, Hipponensis episcopi* is found in J. P. Migne, *Patrologia Latina*, XXXII, 33-578. A revision of this text and an English translation of it, with introduction and notes, were made by H. T. Weiskotten, *Sancti Augustini vita scripta a Possidio Episcopo* (Princeton: Princeton University Press, 1919). In his biography Possidius gives a brief summary of the life of Augustine up to the time of his conversion, and a detailed account of his daily life, work, and character from his ordination to the priesthood until his death in 430 A.D. In this work we have an accurate picture of Augustine as priest and bishop, since Possidius was peculiarly fitted for the task, as he himself expresses it, 'of setting forth the origin, career, and end of this venerable man as I have learned them from him and observed them through so many years of loving friendship.'[32] At the close of his biography he tells us that he lived with Augustine 'on terms of intimate and delightful friendship, with no bitter disagreement, for almost forty years.'[33] Hence, it would seem that we have reason to consider the first-hand information given us by Possidius as authentic.

Other biographies of St. Augustine in English are found in: V. J. Bourke, *Augustine's Quest for Wisdom*, (Milwaukee: Bruce, 1945); C. H. Collette, *St. Augustine—A Sketch of His Life and Writings* (London: W. H. Allen, 1883); L. Bertrand, *Saint Augustine* (New York: D. Appleton Co., 1914), a translation of L. Bertrand, *Saint Augustine* (Paris: A. Fayard, 1913); C. Dawson, 'St. Augustine and His Age,' in *A Monument to St. Augustine*, pp. 11-77 (London: Sheed and Ward, 1930); J. McCabe, *St. Augustine and His Age* (New York: G. Putnam's Sons, 1903); W. Montgomery, *Saint Augustine, Aspects of His Life and Thought* (New York: Hodder and Stoughton, 1914).

B. Editions of Augustine's Writings

The most usual text of the *Opera omnia* of St. Augustine is that edited by the Benedictines of St. Maur, and printed in J. P. Migne, *Patrologia Latina*, T. XXXII-XLVII (Paris: Garnier Bros., 1877-1890). A critical edition of a considerable number of Augustine's writings compiled by various editors is found in the *Corpus scriptorum ecclesiasticorum Latinorum* (Vienna: A. G. Tempsky, 1896-1913).

The most important editions of Augustine's works in English are *The Works of Aurelius Augustine*, 15 vols., edited by M. Dods (Edinburgh: T. and T. Clark, 1871-1874); and *The Nicene and Post-Nicene Fathers of the Christian Church*, vols. I-VIII, first series, edited by P. Schaff (Buffa-

---

[32] Possidius, *Vita sancti Aurelii Augustini, Hipponensis Episcopi*, Preface.
[33] *Ibid.*, c. XXXI.

lo: The Christian Literature Co., 1886-1888). Neither edition includes the complete works of Augustine. The former contains the translation of the *City of God*, the *Letters*, and the doctrinal and moral treatises; the latter, the *Confessions, Soliloquia, City of God*, 160 *Letters* and the doctrinal and moral treatises.

C. *Contra Academicos*

Two incunabula of *Contra Academicos* are extant. Both are found in codices of the *Opuscula plurima* of St. Augustine, which are mentioned in the *Gesamtkatalog der Wiegendrucke*, III, 76-79 (Leipzig: K. W. Hersemann, 1928); in M. Pellechet, *Catalogue général des incunables des bibliothèques publiques de France*, I, 341-342 (Paris: A. Picard et Fils, 1897); and in L. F. Hain, *Repertorium bibliographicum*, I, 245 (Stuttgart and Paris, 1826). The first of these incunabula is in: Augustinus Aurelius, *Opuscula*, edited by Eusebius Conradus and Thaddeus Ugoletus (Parma: Angelus Ugoletus, March 31, 1491. 2°. The second is in: Augustinus Aurelius, *Opuscula* (Venice: Peregrino Pasquale, November 10, 1491). 4°.

The *Contra Academicos* is also found in *Sancti Aureli Augustini opera omnia*, edited by the Benedictines of St. Maur, and printed in J. P. Migne, *Patrologia Latina*, XXXII, 906-957 (Paris: Garnier Bros., 1877). A critical edition of the Latin text comprises Section I, Part III, of the *Corpus scriptorum ecclesiasticorum Latinorum*, edited by Pius Knöll (Vienna: A. G. Tempsky, 1922), pp. 1-81; this is the text used as a basis of the following translation. In the "Ancient Christian Writers" series the *Contra Academicos* has been translated and annotated by J. J. O'Meara, *St. Augustine: Against the Academics*, (Westminister, Md.: The Newman Press, 1950).

A study of the *Contra Academicos* with emphasis on the similarity in content between it and the writings of Cicero is found in P. Drewniok, *De Augustini contra Academicos libri III* (Breslau, 1913), and in C. Thiaucourt, *Les "Academiques" de Cicero et Le "contra Academicos" de saint Augustin* (Paris, 1903). One may also consult the author's *Saint Augustine: Christian or Neo-Platonist?* (Milwaukee: Marquette University Press, 1939), pp. 78-87 and *passim*.

D. Suggested Books on St. Augustine's Philosophy

A general exposition of Augustine's philosophy is contained in: C. Boyer, *Essais sur la doctrine de Saint Augustin* (Paris, 1931); P. De Labriolle, 'Augustin d'Hippone' in *Dictionnaire d'histoire et la géographie ecclesiastique*, V, 440-473 (Paris: Letouzey et Ané, 1931); R. Eucken, *Die Lebensanschauungen der grossen Denker*, (18th Edition; Leipzig, 1922); E. Gilson, *Introduction à l'étude de S. Augustin*, 2d éd. (Paris: J. Vrin, 1949); J. Martin, *Saint Augustin*, (second edition; Paris: F. Alcan,

1923) ; J. F. Nourrisson, *La Philosophie de Saint Augustin,* vol. I (Paris: Didier et Cie, 1865) ; E. Portalié, 'Saint Augustin' in *Dictionnaire de théologie catholique,* I, 2268-2472 (Paris: Letouzey et Ané, 1903).

The following works in English also present a general aspect of Augustine's thought: W. Cunningham, *St. Augustine and His Place in the History of Christian Thought* (London: C. J. Clay and Sons, 1886) ; M. D'Arcy, 'The Philosophy of St. Augustine,' in *A Monument to Saint Augustine,* pp. 155-196 (London: Sheed and Ward, 1930) ; J. F. Spalding, *The Teaching and Influence of Saint Augustine. An Essay with Particular Reference to Recent Misapprehensions* (New York: J. Pott, 1886) ; A. C. Vega, O.S.A., *Saint Augustine, His Philosophy,* translated from the Spanish by D. J. Kavanaugh, O.S.A. (Philadelphia: The Peter Reilly Co., 1931).

Excellent bibliographies on the life and various phases of the philosophy of St. Augustine are found in M. De Wulf, *History of Mediaeval Philosophy,* (third edition, translated from the sixth French edition by E. C. Messenger ; New York: Longmans & Co., 1935), I, 94-100; also in E. Gilson, *Introduction à l'étude de S. Augustin,* 2d éd. (Paris: J. Vrin, 1949), pp. 325-351. F. Van Steenberghen, 'La philosophie de Saint Augustin d'après les travaux du Centenaire' in *Revue Néo-Scholastique, XXXIV* (1932), 386-387 ; XXXV (1933), 106-126, 230-281, contains a good bibliography of the works written in commemoration of the fifteenth centenary of the death of St. Augustine. There is also a treatment of St. Augustine in E. Gilson, *The History of Christian Philosophy in the Middle Ages,* (New York: Random House, 1955), pp. 70-81, bibliography nad notes, pp. 590-596.

SAINT AUGUSTINE

AGAINST THE ACADEMICIANS

FIRST BOOK

I. 1. O Romanianus,[1] if only courage were able to bear away from adverse fortune man who is well qualified for this virtue, in the same way as it allows no one to be removed from itself by ill-luck, it would long ago have laid hands on you, proclaiming you justly as its very own and, by guiding you into the possession of lasting goods, it would not permit you to care even for good fortune. But since it has been arranged either in proportion to our merits or by the necessity of nature,[2] that the mind which is of divine origin can by no means, while clinging to perishable things, be admitted into the harbor of wisdom where it is unmoved either by the favorable or the adverse breath of fortune, unless this favorable or quasi-adverse fortune of itself should lead the mind to this harbor, all we can do for you is to implore that God Who is ever mindful of your needs will restore you to yourself—for in this way He will restore you to us—and that He will permit that mind of yours, which has been pausing for a long time to take breath, to come forth into the breezes of true liberty. For perhaps what is usually called fortune[3] is directed by a certain hidden Providence and we call it nothing else but chance when the reason for it is unknown; and nothing, whether it be of advantage or disadvantage, happens in part which does not harmonize with the whole. Philosophy, to which I am now inviting you, promises to show its true lovers the meaning of the most prolific teachings compiled by the oracles and far removed from the minds of the uninitiated. Therefore, though many things are happening to you not in accordance with your liking, do not neglect yourself. For if Divine

---

[1] The wealthy patron and friend who assisted Augustine with encouragement and financial aid at crucial moments of his life. Cf. *Contra Academicos*, II, ii, 3; *Confessiones*, VI, xiv, 24.

[2] Augustine has reference to the corruption of human nature, which resulted from the sin of Adam. Cf. *Retractationes*, I, i, 3: '. . . satis erat dicere: pro meritis nostris, sicut verum est ex Adam tracta miseria, nec addere: *sive pro necessitate naturae*, quando quidem naturae nostrae dura necessitas merito praecedentis iniquitatis exorta est.'

[3] In *Retractationes*, I, i, 2, Augustine expresses regret for his frequent use of the word *fortune*, since men, he observes, have acquired the undesirable habit of saying 'hoc voluit fortuna,' whereas they ought to say 'hoc Deus voluit.' Whenever he uses the word, he explains, he has no reference to any goddess but rather to the fortuitous outcome of events, whether favorable or otherwise, which, however, is absolutely under the guidance of Divine Providence.

The word *fortuna* is used nine times in the three books of the *Contra Academicos*, cf. I, i, 9; I, ix, 25; II, i, 1; II, iii, 9; III, ii, 2-4.

Providence extends even to us—which is absolutely certain—take my word for it, you are being treated according to your deserts. For while you, a person endowed with such great talents that I often marvel at them, from the beginning of your youth up to the present time have been entering a life filled with all kinds of error along the weak and unaided path of reason, an abundance of riches which seemed attractive has followed you, and they would have engulfed you into their alluring whirlpools if those blasts of fortune which are considered unfavorable had not snatched you when you were almost being submerged.

2. If, indeed, you had received the enthusiastic applause of the theatre when you provided bear hunts as a gift to the people, and spectacles such as had never before been witnessed by our citizens; if you were raised to the very heavens by the shouts of foolish men unanimous in your praise— the number of such men is very great; if no one dared to be unfriendly to you; if the records of the municipal towns designated you the protector not only of their citizens, but also of their neighbors, by erecting bronze tablets in your honor; if statues of you were set up; if honors were showered upon you and civic offices were given you which would increase your standing in politics; if the most delicious viands were served you at daily banquets; if whatever was necessary for anyone, whatever pleasures anyone could desire were sought and thoroughly enjoyed, and many favors were con- ferred upon you even by persons from whom you were not seeking them; if your household carefully and properly managed by your servants, should prove itself well-qualified and should give evidence that it was kept up at great expense; if, in the meantime, you were living in palatial build- ings, in the splendor of the Baths, in mosaics which even men of worth do not despise; if you were enjoying hunting and banquets; if you were men- tioned by your clients, by your fellow citizens, in fact, by the people at large as a most cultured, most generous, most upright, and most fortunate man, would anyone, I ask you, Romanianus, dare to make mention to you of another happy life, which is in reality the only happy one? Would any- one be able to persuade you not only that you are not happy, but that you are extremely unhappy in this very respect in which you seem to yourself to be least so? But now the many and great reverses which you have en- dured have made it possible to give you a little advice. For you do not need to be convinced from the examples of others as to how fleeting, how unstable, how replete with disasters are all those things which mortals consider good, since you have had such experience with them that we can convince others by citing your case.

3. Therefore, a secret Providence has decreed by those various and heavy reverses to awaken within you that divine quality which has been lulled to sleep by the lethargy of this world—that quality by which you

[15]

have always been wont to desire what is fitting and honorable, by which you have preferred to be generous rather than rich, by which you have never desired to be more powerful rather than more just, by which you have never yielded to misfortune or degeneracy. Wake up, wake up, I entreat you. Take my word for it, you will greatly rejoice, because the gifts of this world by which the unwary are enslaved are attractive to you even though you have almost completely lost them. They strove to ensare me also while I was daily singing their praises, if the pain in my chest had not forced me to cast aside my empty profession[4] and to flee to the bosom of philosophy. Now she nourishes and supports me with that peace which we have greatly desired and she has freed me entirely from that fanaticism into which I had cast you headlong with myself.[5] For she teaches— and teaches rightly—that nothing at all should be cherished and that everything should be despised which mortal eye can see, or any sense can appropriate. She promises that she will clearly make known the true and invisible God, and now and again she deigns to show Him to us, as it were, through the bright clouds.[6]

4. Our Licentius[7] who is living with me is very much interested in philosophy. He has turned away completely from the alluring pleasures of youth and is so devoted to her that I would not dare to place him before his father for imitation. For it is philosophy from whose bosom no age can complain that it is excluded. Although I well know your thirst for her, still I have wanted to send you merely a taste in order to make you more eager to cling to and thoroughly enjoy her. I ask that this may be most agreeable to you and prove an inducement, so to speak, so that I may not have hoped in vain. I have sent you in writing a discussion which was carried on between Trygetius and Licentius. For military service would have laid claim upon the former youth also to take away, as it were, his great dislike for learning; so philosophy restored him to us and made him most enthusiastic and eager for the great and liberal arts. Therefore, a few days after we had begun to live in the country when I, while urging and encouraging them to study, saw that they were ready and even desirous to do so beyond my expectation, I wished to try them at something suited to their age,

---

[4] Cf. *De beata vita,* I, 4; *Confessiones,* IX, ii, 2; IX, v, 13.
[5] Augustine seems to have led Romanianus into Manichaeism when he himself became involved in its errors. *Epistulae,* XXVII, 5, would lead us to believe that Romanianus also was converted.
[6] In his early treatises Augustine bestows excessive praise upon philosophy and the philosophic life. In this passage, *Contra Academicos,* I, i, 3, he enthusiastically cites his own case as an illustration of the benefits to be derived from a life devoted to philosophy. Cf. *Contra Academicos,* II, i, 1; III, ii, 3; *De beata vita,* I, 1-2; *De ordine,* I, iii, 9; I. viii, 21; I, xi, 31.
[7] The son of Romanianus and pupil of Augustine. He and Trygetius, also a pupil of Augustine, take part in most of the dialogues written at Cassiciacum.

especially since Cicero's book *Hortensius*[8] seemed already to have attracted them greatly to philosophy. And so, by employing a stenographer, lest the breezes should destroy our labor, I allowed nothing to be lost.[9] In this book, then, you will read the subjects discussed and the opinions of those two young men; also my words and those of Alypius.[10]

II. 5. When, therefore, at my request we had all assembled in one place which seemed suitable for this purpose, I said, 'Have you any doubt at all that we ought to know the truth?' 'By no means,' answered Trygetius, and the others showed by the expression on their faces that they agreed with him. 'But,' I said, 'if we can be happy even if we do not know the truth, do you think that knowledge of the truth is necessary?' Hereupon Alypius replied, 'I think it would be safer for me to be a judge of this discussion. For, since I have planned a journey to the city, I ought to be relieved of the burden of taking any part because I can at any time assign the rôle of judge to someone else more easily than that of anyone's defense. So from now on do not expect me to say anything on either side of the question.' When everyone had granted him this concession and I had again repeated the proposition, Trygetius said, 'We certainly wish to be happy[11] and, if we can attain this happiness without the truth, we do not need to seek the truth.' 'What about this?' I replied. 'Do you think we can be happy even if we have not found the truth?' Then Licentius answered, 'We can if we are seeking the truth.' When I hereupon nodded to the others to express their opinion, Navigius[12] said, 'What Licentius said has impressed me for perhaps it can be said that to live happily is to live in search of the truth.' Trygetius replied, 'Then define what a happy life is so that I may infer from your definition what answer I should give.' 'What do you think?' I said; 'is to live happily anything else except to live according to

---

[8] A treatise written by Cicero to justify the series of philosophic writings which he intended to produce. The work, consisting of two books, is now lost except for a few fragments the most important of which are found in Augustine's own works. Cf. *De beata vita*, III, 10; *Contra Academicos*, I, ii, 5; III, xiv, 31; *Soliloquia*, I, 17; *De civitate Dei*, III, 15; *De Trinitate*, XIII, iv, 7; XIII, v, 8; XIV, ix, 12; XIV, xix, 26; *Epistulae*, cxxx, 10. Augustine probably selected the *Hortensius* in order to arouse within his students a love for philosophy, since the treatise had produced this effect upon him when he read it at the age of nineteen. He acknowledges that it was the *Hortensius* which produced a complete change in his life and views, and which led him to God. Cf. *De beata vita*, I, i, 4; *Confessiones*, III, iv, 7.

[9] Augustine insisted that the arguments developed in the early treatises be taken down in shorthand and later on be written out in full. Cf. *Contra Academicos*, II, ix, 22; also *De ordine*, I, x, 29-30. It would seem that he intended them to be used by his pupils for reference. Cf. *Epistulae*, CLXVII.

[10] An intimate friend of Augustine. He followed Augustine to Milan, accompanied him to Cassiciacum, was converted and baptized at the same time as Augustine. Later he became Bishop of Tagaste. Cf. *Confessiones*, VI, vii, 11; VI, x, 17; VI, xii, 20-21; VII, xix, 25; VIII, viii, 19; VIII, xii, 29 ff; IX, vi, 14.

[11] Cicero, *Hortensius*, fragment 36. Cf. *Tusculanae disputationes*, V, x, 28.

[12] Augustine's brother. He is also mentioned in *De beata vita*, I, i, 6; *De ordine*, I, iii, 7. *Confessiones*, IX, xi, 27.

that which is best in man?' 'I shall not answer at random,' he replied; 'for I think 'what is best' should be defined for me.' 'Who would doubt,' I answered 'that nothing else is best in man than that part of the soul to which it is fitting that all other things which are in man should submit as to their ruler? But lest you demand another definition, that (part) can be called the *mens* or reason.[13] If you do not agree with this, think out how you yourself would define either a happy life, or what is best in man.' 'I agree,' he said.

6. 'What then? To return to our proposition,' I said, 'do you think one can live happily if he is merely in search of truth and has not found it?' 'I repeat that same opinion of mine,' he answered, 'I by no means think it possible.' 'What do the rest of you think?' I said. Then Licentius spoke: 'It seems to me that he certainly can. For our ancestors whom we have considered wise and happy lived well and happily for this reason only, because they were seeking the truth.' 'I am grateful,' I said, 'that you have made me a judge along with Alypius whom, I confess, I had begun to envy. Since, then, it seems to one of you that a happy life is attained solely by the search for truth, and to the other that it consists only in finding the truth, and since Navigius stated a little while ago that he wished to be converted to your opinion, Licentius, I shall observe with great interest what kind of defenders of your opinions you will prove to be. For the subject is an important one and is most deserving of a careful discussion.' 'If the subject is important,' said Licentius, 'it requires able men.' 'Do not demand, especially in this villa, what it is difficult to find anywhere in the world,' I replied, 'but explain rather why this opinion has been expressed by you not thoughtlessly, as I think, and by what process of reasoning it seems to you to be true. For subjects of very great importance when investigated by persons who are inexperienced are accustomed to make them capable.'

III. 7. He answered, 'Since I see you insist on our discussing both sides of this argument, I shall ask a question which I trust you will consider helpful—why he can not be happy who is seeking the truth, even if he should by no means find it.' 'Because,' replied Trygetius, 'we consider the happy man as possessing perfect wisdom in all things. But he who is still in search of something is not perfect. I do not see at all, then, how you can claim that he is happy.' Licentius said, 'Can the authority of our ancestors have any weight with you?' 'Not of all of them,' replied Trygetius.

---

[13] In the *Retractationes,* I, i, 5, Augustine thus explains and completes the definition here given for a happy life: 'Hoc quidem verum—nam quantum adtinet ad hominis naturam, nihil est in eo melius quam meus et ratio—sed non secundum ipsam debet vivere, qui beate vult vivere. Alioquin secundum hominem vivit, cum secundum deum vivendum sit, ut possit ad beatitudinem pervenire, propter quam consequendam non se ipsa debet esse contenta, sed deo mens nostra subdenda est.'

'Of which among them, then?' said Licentius. Trygetius replied, 'Of those, indeed, who were wise.' 'Does Carneades[14] seem to you to be wise?' asked Licentius. 'I am not a Greek,' replied Trygetius, 'I do not know who that Carneades was.' 'Then what do you think about that Cicero of ours?' said Licentius. After remaining silent for a long time, Trygetius answered, 'He was a wise man.' 'Then has his opinion in regard to this matter some weight with you?' asked Licentius. 'It has,' his opponent replied. 'Then listen to what it is, for I think you have forgotten it,' remarked Licentius. 'Our Cicero was of the opinion that he is happy who is in search of the truth even if he cannot find it.'[15] Trygetius asked, 'Where did Cicero say this?' And Licentius replied, 'Who does not know that he stated emphatically that nothing can be apprehended by man, and nothing can persist for a wise man except a painstaking search for truth because, if any assent were given to uncertain matters, even though they might perhaps be true, there could be no freedom from error, which is the greatest fault in a wise man. Therefore if we must believe that a wise man is necessarily happy and if only the search for truth is unquestionably the function of wisdom, why do we hesitate to think that a happy life even by itself is possible by the mere seeking for truth?'

8. Then Trygetius asked, 'Is it permitted us to return to what has been granted without due deliberation?' I replied, 'They are not accustomed to grant this who are led into an argument not through a desire of finding the truth, but for the childish purpose of displaying their ability. Therefore, as far as I am concerned, especially since you are still to be trained and instructed, I not only grant the permission but I also wish to enjoin upon you the importance of returning during a discussion to any points which you may have rather thoughtlessly admitted.' Licentius added, 'I think that is of no little advantage in philosophy when a victory is considered of little account by the disputant in comparison with finding out what is right and true. And so I shall gladly comply with your injunction and follow your recommendation and permit Trygetius to return to what he thinks he has rashly conceded—for this privilege belongs to me.' Then Alypius said, 'You recall that I have not yet performed my part of the duty which I took upon myself. But since my departure which was arranged some time ago forces me to interrupt your argument, my associate judge here will not refuse the double power conferred upon him until my return; for I see that this contest of yours will continue somewhat longer.' When he had departed, Licentius continued, 'What did you rashly concede? Mention it.' Trygetius replied, 'I thoughtlessly said that Cicero was wise.' 'Then,' said

---

[14] Carneades was the most important representative of the New Academy in Athens, toward whose doctrine Augustine leaned for a time after having renounced Manichaeism. Cf. *Confessiones*, V, x, 19.
[15] Cf. Cicero, *Hortensius*, fragment 101.

Licentius, 'was Cicero not wise, the man by whom philosophy was begun and completed in the Latin language?'[16] 'Even if I grant that he was wise,' replied Trygetius, 'still I do not approve of all his teachings.' 'Then you ought to reject many other statements of his, that it may not seem presumptuous in you to disapprove of this doctrine which we are now discussing,' said Licentius. Trygetius answered, 'What if I am prepared to prove that this is the only doctrine which he did not understand correctly? Your opinion, I believe, is of no importance unless I can produce reasons of some weight for claiming what I wish.' 'Go ahead, then,' said Licentius, 'for what should I dare to say in opposition to him who acknowledges himself an opponent of Cicero?'

9. Hereupon Trygetius said, 'I wish that you, our judge, would assist us in defining a happy life more clearly; for you said that he is happy who lives according to that part of the soul which it is fitting should command the others. But I wish that you, Licentius, would now admit that he is not perfect who is still seeking truth—for I have already cast aside the yoke of authority because of the freedom to which philosophy promises in a special way to conduct us.' After a long silence Licentius said, 'I do not grant that.' 'But explain why, I entreat you,' replied Trygetius; 'for I am extremely interested and most eager to hear how man can both be perfect and still be seeking truth.' Then Licentius said, 'I confess that he who has not reached his goal is not perfect. However, I think that God alone knows that truth or perhaps the soul of man when it has left this dark prison of the body.[17] But the end of man is to seek truth perfectly; for we are seeking a perfect being, but nevertheless a human being.' And Trygetius replid, 'Therefore man cannot be happy for how can he be since he is unable to attain what he greatly desires? But man can live happily if indeed he can live according to that part of the soul which it is fitting should rule in man. Therefore he can find truth, or he should practice self-control and not desire truth lest, since he cannot attain it, he should necessarily be unhappy.' 'But in this very thing consists the happiness of man,' said Licentius, 'in seeking truth wholeheartedly; for this is what it means to reach the goal beyond which he cannot advance. Whoever, therefore, seeks truth less earnestly than he ought, does not attain the end of man; but whoever does his best at finding truth in so far as man can and ought, even if he does not find it, is happy; for he does everything which he was intended by nature to do. But if he still lacks finding the truth, he lacks that which nature has not given him.

---

[16] Evidently Augustine had instilled his own profound admiration for Cicero into the hearts of his pupils. Cicero made no claim to originality in philosophy. He seems to have regarded himself merely as an interpreter of the Greek systems of which he treats. Cf. *Academica,* I, i, 3.

[17] This statement bears evidence of Platonic and Neo-Platonic influence on Augustime, at least, on his terminology. Cf. Plato, *Gorgias,* 493A; *Cratylus,* 400C. Also Plotinus, *Enneads,* II, ix, 7; IV, viii, 4.

Finally, since it is necessary for man to be either happy or unhappy, is it not the act of a fool to call him unhappy who persists in seeking truth night and day in so far as he is able? Therefore he will be happy. That definition then, as I see it, recommends itself to me as being quite comprehensive; for if he is happy, as he certainly is, who lives according to that part of his soul which it is fitting should rule the others, and that part is called reason, I ask you whether he does not live according to reason who is seeking truth perfectly. If this is unreasonable, why do we hesitate to say that man is happy solely by seeking truth?'

10. Trygetius said, 'It seems to me that anyone who is in error neither lives according to reason nor is really happy. But everyone is in error who is always seeking but does not find that for which he seeks. Therefore you must prove one of these two statements: that a person can be happy who is in error, or that he who never finds what he is seeking is not in error.' Then Licentius replied, 'A happy man cannot be in error.' And after a long silence he added, 'But he is not in error when he is seeking, because he is seeking in order not to be in error.' 'He is, indeed, seeking,' answered Trygetius, 'that he may not be in error, but, when he does not at all find that for which he seeks, he is in error. But you thought that the very fact that he does not wish to err would be of advantage to you, just as if no one would err against his will or anyone would err at all if he were not unwilling.' Then when Licentius hesitated a long time in making a reply, I said, 'You ought to define what error is, for then you can more easily consider the exact meaning of that term with which you are now deeply concerned.' Licentius said, 'I am not capable of defining anything, although it is easier to set limits to the meaning of error than to determine the exact scope of the term.' 'I,' said Trygetius, 'shall define that word which seems very easy to me, not because of my ability but for the very best reason. For surely to err is always to seek and never to find.' Licentius replied, 'If I were able to refute that definition of yours easily, I would not have failed to settle this difficulty for myself long ago, but since the subject by its very nature is complicated, or at least it appears so to me, I ask you to permit this argument to be postponed until tomorrow, if I do not find it possible to make a reply today, as I should like to ponder over it carefully.' Since I thought this favor should be granted him and the others did not object, we rose up to go for a walk and while we were engaged in various topics of conversation, he was buried in thought. When he perceived that it was to no purpose, he decided to relax his mind and to take part in our conversation. Afterward when it was drawing toward evening, they returned to the disputed question, but I put an end to their discussion and persuaded them to postpone it for another day. Then we went to the Baths.

[21]

11. However, on the following day when we had taken our places, I said, 'Continue what you began yesterday.' Then Licentius said, 'We postponed the argument, if I am not mistaken, at my request when I found the definition of error very difficult.' Then I remarked, 'You are not wholly in error because I desired very much that you should have an augury (omen)[18] for your remaining arguments.' 'Listen, then,' he said, 'to what I would have stated yesterday if you had not prevented me. Error, it seems to me, is the assent to what is false instead of what is true. It can in no way befall anyone who thinks that the truth should always be sought; for he who approves of nothing cannot approve of what is false; therefore he cannot be in error. Moreover, he can very easily be happy; for, not to go any further away, if we were permitted to live every day as it was granted us yesterday, I see no reason why we should hesitate to call ourselves happy. For we lived in great peace of mind, preserving our souls from every corporal stain and far removed from passionate desires, devoting ourselves, in so far as a human being can, to reason, that is, living in accordance with that divine part of the soul in which a happy life consists, according to our definition yesterday; and yet, I believe, we found nothing, but merely sought the truth. Therefore man can attain happiness merely by seeking the truth even though he can by no means find it. For see how easily your definition may be distinguished from the common notion. For you said that to err is always to seek and never to find. What about this, if anyone should seek nothing and were asked, for example, whether it is day, and for the time being he mistakenly thinks and replies that it is night, do you not think he is in error? Therefore your definition has not included this or most ordinary kind of error. Indeed, can any definition be more faulty if it does not even include those involved in error? For if anyone were seeking Alexandria and proceeding toward it along the right road, I do not think you can say he is in error. Why, if he should continue on this same road for a long time, though retarded for various reasons, and if death should overtake him while he was still on his journey, did he not constantly seek and never find and, nevertheless, was not in error?' Trygetius replied, 'He did not constantly seek.'

12. 'What you say is correct and your advice is good,' said Licentius. 'Then your definition is certainly not pertinent; for I did not say that he is happy who is always seeking the truth. Indeed, this is not even possible because, in the first place, man does not live forever, and, secondly, he can not even seek the truth from the time at which he begins to live since the immaturity of early years prevents him from so doing. If you think the

---

[18] In the *Retractationes*, I, 1, 16, Augustine remarks that he used the word *omen* merely by way of jest. He would be unwilling, he says, to use such a term seriously as it does not appear 'sive in sacris Litteris nostris, sive in sermone cujusquam ecclesiastici disputatoris.'

word always should be used, if he does not allow a moment to be lost from the time at which he is able to seek, you ought to return to Alexandria again. For grant that anyone, from the time that his age or business permits him to make the journey, begins to go along the road and, as I said before, although he never deviates from it, still he dies before he arrives at his destination, you will, indeed, be mistaken if you think he has erred even though he did not cease seeking it every moment he could, and yet was not able to reach the place toward which he was advancing. Therefore if my interpretation is correct and, according to it, he is not in error who is seeking the truth perfectly even though he should not discover it, and he is happy from the very fact that he is living according to reason, then your definition is rejected and even if it were not, I ought not pay any attention to it, if the case has been proved solely from the definition which I gave; why, then, I ask, has the subject of discussion between us not yet been cleared up?'

V. 13. Hereupon Trygetius spoke: 'Do you grant that wisdom is the right way of life?' 'I certainly do,' Licentius answered, 'but still I should like you to define wisdom so I may know whether my interpretation of the word is the same as yours.' Trygetius replied, 'Don't you think it was defined well enough by the very question which you were just asked? You also admitted what I desired. For, if I am not mistaken, wisdom is called the right way of life.' Then Licentius said, 'Nothing seems so absurd to me as that definition of yours.' 'Perhaps it does,' said Trygetius, 'nevertheless I shall carefully strive to make reason anticipate your ridicule; for nothing is more odious than ridicule which deserves to be laughed at.' 'Well then,' Licentius asked, 'do you not admit that death is the opposite of life?' 'I do,' replied Trygetius. 'Then it seems to me,' said Licentius, 'that the way of life is no other than that by which each one advances, in order that he may avoid death.' Trygetius agreed. Licentius continued, 'Therefore, if any traveler should continue to go along the right way, avoiding a bypath which he had heard was infested with robbers, and in this way should escape death, did he not pursue both the way of life and the right one? And does anyone call this wisdom? How, then, is every right way of life wisdom?' 'I granted it to be that, but not merely that,' said Trygetius. 'But a definition ought not include anything which would be irrelevant. So please define again what you think wisdom is,' Licentius added.

14. Trygetius was silent for a long time and then said, 'Behold, I shall define it again if you are determined not to accept this broad definition. Wisdom is the right way which leads to truth.' Licentius replied, 'I likewise reject this definition. For in Vergil,[19] when Aeneas was told by his mother: 'Only go ahead and direct your steps where the way leads you,'

---

[19] Cf. Vergil, *Aeneidos*, I, 401.

following this path, he arrived at that which was spoken of, that is, at the truth. Prove, if you please, that where he stepped while going can be called wisdom; and yet it is very foolish for me to break down your explanation; for it does not in any way help my cause. For you said that wisdom is not truth itself but the way which leads to truth. Whoever, then, makes use of this way, is indeed using wisdom, and he who uses wisdom is necessarily a wise man; therefore he will be wise who seeks truth perfectly even though he has not yet attained it. For no way which leads to truth, according to my way of thinking, is known better than the diligent search of truth. Therefore, by making use of this way alone, he will already be wise. Now, no wise man is unhappy; but every man is either happy or unhappy; therefore not merely the finding of truth will make man happy but the very search for truth.'

15. Trygetius smilingly answered, 'It is right that such things happen to me when I confidently agree with my adversary on a point which is not essential, as if, indeed, I am capable at defining, or consider anything rather superfluous in arguing. For what limit will there be if I should wish you to define something again and pretending that I do not understand it, I should demand that the words of this same definition and all that would logically follow from them also be defined one by one? For of what word has nature wished us to have a clearer idea than the word wisdom? But somehow when the idea itself has left, as it were, the harbor of our mind and has spread out its sails of words, so to speak, a thousand shipwrecks of accusations forthwith rush upon it. Therefore, either the definition of wisdom must not be demanded, or our judge should deign to come to its defense.' Then since night prevented any further writing, and I saw that a point important for the whole argument, as it were, was ripe for discussion, I postponed it for another day. For it was nearly sunset when we had begun our discussion, and almost the whole day had been spent in putting our country home in order and then in reviewing the first book of Vergil.[20]

16. As soon as daylight appeared—for everything had been arranged the day before so that there might be abundant leisure—a continuation of the discussion was immediately begun. Then I said: 'Yesterday, Trygetius, you requested that I step down from my rôle as judge to make a defense of wisdom, as if, indeed, wisdom would allow any adversary in your discussion or would be in such distress when anyone was defending her, as to find it necessary to beg for more abundant aid. For you have brought up no other subject for inquiry than what is wisdom—a subject on which neither of you will make an attack because both of you desire it—and even

---

[20] At Cassiciacum Augustine spent considerable time with his pupils in reviewing the poetry of Vergil, in which he had taken great delight in his early youth. Cf. *Confessiones*, I, xiii, 20-22; I, xiv, 23.

[24]

if you think you have failed in defining wisdom, you ought not for that reason abandon the rest of the defense of your opinion. So you will get nothing else from me except a definition of wisdom which is neither my own nor is it new; it is the definition of our ancestors and I am surprised that you do not remember it. For you are not hearing now for the first time that wisdom is the knowledge of things both human and divine.'[21]

17. Hereupon Licentius, who I thought would have a question to ask after this definition, immediately added: 'Why, then, I ask, do we not call that profligate man wise who, we know well, is wont to be charged with all kinds of debaucheries, I mean that notorious Albicerius who gave such astonishing and correct answers to those who consulted him for many years at Carthage? I could mention a number of examples if I were not speaking to those who are familiar with them; so a few will now be sufficient for my purpose. When a spoon was lost at home—he told me about this case—and he was asked by your orders the name of the article which was being sought, to whom it belonged, and where it was hidden, did he not answer very truly and rapidly? Also in my presence—I pass over the fact that he was by no means mistaken in regard to that which was asked—but when a boy who was carrying coins had stolen some of them and we referred the matter to Albicerius, he ordered all the coins to be counted for him and he forced the boy, before our very eyes, to return those which he had taken, before he himself had even seen these same coins or had heard from us how much had been brought to him.

18. What of the fact that we have heard from you, that the learned and illustrious man Flaccianus was wont to be astonished who, after having spoken about buying a farm, reported the matter to that divinely inspired man to see if Albicerius were able to tell him what he had done? And he immediately made known not only the nature of the business, but also the very name of the farm in regard to which he expressed himself in terms of great admiration, although the name was so ridiculous that Flaccianus himself had scarcely remembered it. Even now I cannot mention without astonishment the reply which Albicerius gave our friend, your pupil, who, wishing to confuse him, boldly demanded that he should tell him what he himself was thinking about; he replied that he [your pupil] was thinking about a verse from Vergil. When he, greatly astonished, could not deny it and hastened to inquire what the verse was, Albicerius, who had scarcely ever seen in passing, the school of a grammarian, with great unconcern and in a loud tone of voice did not hesitate to recite the verse. Therefore, were these not human affairs about which he was consulted or did he make such correct and true replies to those who were questioning him, without the

---

[21] This definition was formulated by Cicero. Cf. *Tusculanae disputationes,* IV, xxvi, *27*; *De officiis,* II, 5.

knowledge of divine matters? But either case is absurd. For human matters are nothing else than the affairs of men, such as silver, coins, a farm, and finally even thought itself, and who would not rightly think that divine matters are those through which divination is granted to men? Therefore Albicerius[22] was a wise man if we admit, according to that definition, that wisdom is the knowledge of things both human and divine.'

19. Then Trygetius replied: 'In the first place, I do not call that knowledge in which he who professes it is at any time deceived. For knowledge consists not only in comprehending things, but in comprehending them in such a way that no one should be in error in regard to it nor be uncertain when hard pressed by any adversaries. Whence the statement has been truly made by certain philosophers, that knowledge can be found in no one except a wise man who should not only have perfect command of what he supports and follows, but should also cling to it truly and firmly. But we know that he whom you mentioned, often said many things that were not true, a fact which I have learned not only from others who reported it to me, but which I myself sometimes witnessed. Should I call him, then, a learned man since he often said what was not true, if I would not consider him learned who spoke the truth in a hesitating manner? Remember, I have been speaking in regard to soothsayers, augurs, and all those who consult the stars, and also interpreters of dreams; or produce, if you can, from among this class of men anyone who, when consulted, never hesitated in giving an answer and, finally, who never made a false reply. For I do not think I need to be concerned with soothsayers who express thoughts which are not their own.

20. Then, to grant that human affairs are the possessions of men, do you think anything really belongs to us, which fortune can either give or take away from us? Or when knowledge of human affairs is spoken of, is reference made to that knowledge by which each of us knows how many or what kind of farms he has, what gold or silver he possesses, or, finally, what unrelated ideas he may be thinking of? That is knowledge of human affairs, which knows the light of prudence, the glory of self-control, the strength of courage, the sacredness of justice. For these are possessions which we rightly dare to call our own without any fear of chance; if Albicerius possessed this kind of knowledge, take my word for it, he would not have led such a dissolute and licentious life. Moreover, I do not think that the fact of his saying, when consulted, whatever verse his inquirer was thinking of should be included among our possessions, not that I would

---

[22] Divination and astrology seem to have been practiced quite commonly in Carthage at the time of Augustine. In *Confessiones,* IV, iii, 4-5, he tells us that he himself consulted astrologers and put faith in them notwithstanding the arguments of the learned physician, Vindicianus, and of his friend, Nebridius, who tried to dissuade him from this evil practice.

deny that creditable teachings may be considered a certain possession of our mind, but because it has been admitted that he also uttered a verse which was unfamiliar to most inexperienced men. When such things happen to come into our mind, it is not strange, since they can be known by some of the most worthless beings of the air whom they call demons, who, I admit, surpass us in keenness and subtlety of observation, but not in reason; this occurs in some manner that is unknown and far removed from our power of apprehension. For even if we wonder that a little bee after putting away its honey, flies to it again and again with a sagacity which surpasses that of man, we ought not for that reason prefer it to or even compare it with ourselves.

21. Therefore I should prefer that this Albicerius be asked by him who wished to test his knowledge, whether he had ever taught poetic metres, or that this same Albicerius be forced by someone consulting him, to sing appropriate verses on a subject assigned him at the very moment. You are wont to recall that this same Flaccianus often said this when he was ridiculing and expressing his contempt for that kind of divination with its great secrecy and when he attributed it to some kind of a vile soul—for this is what he called it; it was by the assistance and inspiration of this spirit, as it were, that Albicerius was accustomed to give his replies. For that most learned man inquired of those who wondered at such ability whether Albicerius was able to teach grammar, music, or geometry. But who that knew him would not confess that he was absolutely ignorant of all these studies? Therefore he finally urged them by all means to prefer their own minds which had learned such branches of knowledge to that kind of divination, and to endeavor to improve their minds by training and to strengthen their intellect by which it was possible to pass beyond and soar above the aerial nature of invisible beings.

22. But now, since, as all admit, divine matters are of a higher order and are much more sublime than human affairs, how could he attain a knowledge of them, who did not know what he himself was, unless, perhaps, he thought that the stars which we daily observe are a subject of great importance in comparison with the most true and invisible God Whom the intellect rarely, and Whom the senses never touch? But these things are present to our eyes; they are not, therefore, those divine matters such as wisdom maintains that she alone knows. But the other things which some men who practise divination make use of, either for vain boasting or for profit, are certainly more worthless when compared with the stars. Albicerius, therefore, had no share in the knowledge of things human and divine, and so in that respect our definition was attacked by you in vain. Finally, since we ought to consider most useless, and absolutely despise whatever is contrary to things human and divine, I ask you, in what mat-

ters does that wise man of yours seek truth?' 'In divine matters,' Licentius replied; 'for virtue even in man certainly is divine.' 'Then did Albicerius know those things which a wise man, according to your way of thinking, will always seek?' asked Trygetius. Licentius then said: 'He knew divine matters but not those which must be sought by a wise man. For who would not overthrow every established usage in speech if he granted divination to him and, at the same time, would take away divine realities from which the word divination is taken? Therefore, if I am not mistaken, that definition of yours included something else which did not pertain to wisdom.'

23. Then Trygetius added, 'He who gave that definition will defend it if he so pleases. But now I should like you to answer a question so we may at least come to the subject of which we are now treating.' 'I am ready for it,' Licentius said. Trygetius asked, 'Do you grant that Albicerius knew the truth?' 'I do,' replied Licentius. 'Then he is better than your wise man,' Trygetius said. 'By no means,' said Licentius, 'for not only that foolish soothsayer, but not even the wise man himself while he lives in this body, attains the kind of truth which the wise man is seeking. And yet it merely amounts to this, that it is much more remarkable to be always seeking the latter kind than at some time to find the former.' Trygetius replied, 'I need that definition to assist me in my difficulties. If it seemed faulty to you because it included him whom we cannot call wise, I ask whether you would approve of this definition, if we should say that wisdom is the knowledge of things human and divine, but of those things which have reference to a happy life.' 'That is wisdom,' answered Licentius, 'but it is not merely that. While the former definition included what is extraneous to wisdom, the latter omitted what intrinsically belongs to the term; therefore the former can be used in reference to avarice and the latter, to folly. But now to explain by a definition what I understand by the term, it seems to me that wisdom is not merely the knowledge of things human and divine which refer to a happy life, but also a diligent search for it. If you should wish to subdivide this definition, the first part, which comprises the knowledge, pertains to God; but that part which is satisfied with seeking, belongs to man. In respect to the former, God is happy; in respect to the latter, man is.' Trygetius then said: 'I wonder how you can claim that your wise man is spending his efforts in vain.' 'How can he spend his efforts in vain,' replied Licentius, 'when he is seeking with so great a reward in view? For he is wise from the very fact that he is seeking and he is happy from the very fact that he is wise, since he divests his mind, in so far as he can, of all the wrappings of the body[23] and he collects himself within the depths

---

[23] Here again we have evidence of the influence of Platonic and Neo-Platonic doctrine on Augustine in reference to the relation of soul and body in man. Cf. *Contra Academicos,* I, iii, 9.

of his own consciousness, since he does not allow himself to be torn asunder by his passions, but always calmly directs his attention to himself and to God, with the result that both here on earth he enjoys a life directed by reason, in which, we agreed before, his happiness consists, and on the last day of his life he is found ready to attain that which he has eagerly desired, and thus he rightly enjoys divine happiness who has formerly enjoyed human happiness.'

24.   Then when Trygetius was deliberating a long time over what reply he should make, I said: 'I do not think he will lack arguments, Licentius, if we permit him to investigate the subject at his leisure. For did he fail to give a reply at any point in the argument? For example, he himself first inferred, since the question arose concerning a happy life, and since only the happy man can be wise, that if folly is considered an unhappy state even in the judgment of the foolish, then the wise man ought to be perfect; but he is not perfect who is still seeking truth; therefore, he is not even happy. When at this point you opposed the weight of authority, though somewhat disturbed by the name of Cicero, yet he rose to the occasion at once and by noble persistence he leaped to the very peak of liberty and again seized what had been violently torn from his hands, and inquired of you whether you considered a man perfect who was still seeking, with this in mind, that, if you would not admit that he was perfect, he would rush to the important point and show you, if he could, that by your definition man is perfect if he controls his life in accordance with the law of reason and by this very fact he cannot be happy unless he is perfect. When you had extricated yourself from this snare more carefully than I expected you would, and said that the perfect man is one who is most earnestly seeking truth, and when you struggled more confidently and openly by means of that very definition by which we had said that the happy life was, in its last analysis, a life which was spent in accordance with reason, then he simply carried the argument over to you; for he seized your garrison whence you had been routed and had absolutely lost the most strategic point, if a truce had not been granted you. For where have the Academicians, whose opinion you are defending, placed their citadel if not in the definition of error? If this definition did not perchance recur to your mind in sleep, you would not now have any reply to make, since you mentioned this same point before in explaining the opinion of Cicero. Then it came to the definition of wisdom which you tried to weaken with such great cleverness that not even your helper, Albicerius himself, would perhaps understand your tricks since you opposed it with such carefulness, with such force, as to almost overwhelm and crush yourself if you had not finally defended yourself by your new definition and said that human wisdom is the search for truth, which results in a happy life on account of the

[29]

peace of mind which it affords. Trygetius will not make a reply to this opinion, especially if he demands that the favor be granted him in prolonging the day or that portion of it which now remains.

25. But, not to go into any further details, let that discussion of yours be concluded, if you please, since I think it is unnecessary to spend any more time on it. For the subject has been treated sufficiently well for the purpose we had in view; after a few words it could be ended altogether if I did not wish to give you practice and to test your vigor and perseverance, in which I am greatly interested. For when I began to urge you to seek for truth, I took the first step by inquiring what importance you would place upon it; but you all considered it so important that I could not desire anything more. For since we desire to be happy, we must earnestly inquire whether this cannot be attained except by finding truth or by diligently seeking truth, and we should consider all other things of less importance if we wish to be happy. Therefore, as I have said, let us now conclude this argument and let us send a report of it especially to your father, Licentius, whose mind I am now trying hard to direct toward philosophy. However, up to the present time I am still seeking an opportunity to admit him. But he can be more enthusiastically drawn to these pursuits when he learns that you are spending the time with me, not only in listening to but also by taking part in such discussions. But if the Academicians please you, as I believe they do, prepare stronger arguments to defend them; for I have decided to make charges against them.'[24] After I finished speaking, we stood up.

---

[24] Augustine's main objective in the *Contra Academicos* was the refutation of the skepticism of the New Academy as portrayed by Cicero in the *Academica*, and the proof that truth can be attained by man.

SECOND BOOK

I. 1. If it were as necessary to find wisdom when it is being sought, as it is for a wise man to be unable to be so without the training and knowledge of wisdom, all the slander, or obstinacy (pertinacia),[1] or persistency of the Academicians, or, as I sometimes think, the character suited to that age would surely be buried simultaneously with the age itself and with the bodies of Carneades and Cicero.[2] But since men, if they seek wisdom at all, do not seek it diligently, and since they are turned away from the desire of seeking it by the many and various trivialities of this life, as is the case with you, Romanianus, or by a certain insensibility of their mental powers, or by indolence, or by sluggishness of mind, or by despair of ever finding wisdom—because the star of wisdom does not appear so easily before our minds as light does to our eyes—or even by a false conception of truth when it has been discovered by them, an error which is common among people, the result is that knowledge is seldom attained and only by a few people; and from this very fact it happens that the arms of the Academicians, when one meets them in a hand to hand struggle, seem invincible and, as it were, Vulcan-like (Vulcania),[3] not merely to men of ordinary ability, but even to those who are keen-minded and scholarly. Therefore, men should not only struggle against those waves and tempests of fortune with the oars of all kinds of virtues, but they should especially implore the Divine aid with reverence and devotion so that the firm purpose of their good desires may hold its course from which no mishap may drive it, to prevent it from entering the most safe and delightful harbor of philosophy. This first case is yours; it is in this respect that I fear for you, it is from this that I desire you to be set free; it is in this regard, if I am worthy to obtain this favor, that I do not cease to pray every day for favorable breezes for you; moreover, I am entreating the very power and wisdom of the most High God.[4] For what else is it but Him Whom the mysteries reveal to us as Son of God?

2. But you will aid me greatly while I am begging this favor for you, if you will not give up hope that our prayers can be heard and if you will

---

[1] *Pertinacia,* as used by Cicero, seems to have the meaning of perseverance in its bad sense. It is a vice frequently condemned by him. Cf. *De finibus bonorum et malorum,* I, 27, 28; II, 9, 107; *Tusculanae disputationes,* II, 5.

[2] Augustine associates the names of Carneades and Cicero because the latter was in favor of the doctrine of Carneades. Cicero's object in writing the *Academica* was to justify the mitigated skepticism of the New Academy of which Carneades was the most important representative.

[3] Cf. Vergil, *Aeneidos,* VIII, 535; XII, 739.

[4] Cf. I. *Corinthians,* I, 24, in which St. Paul speaks of Christ as the power of God and the wisdom of God.

[31]

strive with us not only by prayer,[5] but also of your own free will, and by that nobility of mind so characteristic of you, on account of which I am seeking you, by which I am particularly delighted, which I am always admiring, which lies within you—sad to say—hidden by those clouds of personal difficulties, a thunderbolt, so to speak, and is unknown to many, to almost everyone, in fact, but it is not concealed from me and two other very intimate friends of yours, who not only have often listened attentively to your murmurings, but also have seen some flashes of lightning preceding the thunder claps. For, to pass over other illustrations for the time being and to mention only one point, whose mind, I say, ever resounded with such unexpected peals of thunder or emitted such a brilliant flame, that the fire of passion raging fiercely within it the day before died out in one day by one crash of reason and one flash of self-control? Therefore will such virtue as that not come to light some time and change the derision of many who are in despair into horror and amazement, and, after speaking on earth about certain indications, as it were, of the future, having cast aside the burden of the body, return again into heaven?[6] Then is it in vain that Augustine has spoken these words about Romanianus? He to whom I have completely devoted myself and whom I am only now beginning to know quite well will not permit that.

II. 3. Therefore, come with me to philosophy; here you will find what is wont to have a marvelous effect on you when you are worried and in doubt. For I have no reason for fear in your case either from the weakness of your character or the slowness of your mind. Who has shown himself more mentally alert in our discussions or of keener judgment than you, when sufficient time was given you to ponder over the subject? Shall I not make some recompense to you for all your kindness? Or rather am I not under obligation to make some little return? In my youth when I, a poor boy, was pursuing my studies, you aided me by the hospitality of your

---

[5] Augustine here stresses the efficacy of the prayer of petition, thereby implying the personal character of God and the personal relation existing between Him and man. This definitely Christian doctrine is a strong argument against those who maintain that in 386 A.D. Augustine was converted to Neo-Platonism and not to Christianity. Cf. especially: P. Alfaric, *L'évolution intellectuelle de saint Augustin. I. Du Manichéisme au Néoplatonisme* (Paris: E. Nourry, 1918); E. Becker, *Augustin, Studien zu seiner geistigen Entwicklung* (Leipzig: J. C. Hinrich, 1908); L. Gourdon, *Essai sur la conversion de saint Augustin* (Paris: A. Coueslant, 1900).

[6] In the *Retractationes* I, i, 3, Augustine explains that in using the word return [*rediturus*] he did not have in mind that human souls have fallen from heaven and have been cast into bodies on account of some sin, but that he had reference to their going back to God, the Author of their being: 'Alio loco de animo, cum agerem dixi: *Securior rediturus in coelum, iturus* autem quam *rediturus* dixissem securius, propter eos qui putant animos humanos pro meritis peccatorum suorum de coelo lapsos sive dejectos, in corpora ista detrudi. Sed hoc ego propterea non dubitavi dicere, quia ita dixi *in coelum*, tanquam dicerem, ad Deum qui ejus est auctor et conditor . . .'

home, by paying my expenses, and, what is more, by the encouragement you gave me; you consoled me by your friendship when I was deprived of my father. You inspired me with confidence; you helped me with money; you made me almost as well known, you placed me almost in the same rank as yourself in our town by your good will, your friendship, by sharing your very home with me. When I disclosed to you alone among all my friends my hope and intention of returning to Carthage to seek a more brilliant career, although you hesitated somewhat on account of your innate love for your native city, because I was teaching there at that time, yet when you were unable to prevail upon the passionate desire of a youth who was striving for what seemed better, you turned from the rôle of a dissuader to that of a helper by your extraordinary moderation and kindness. You provided me with everything necessary for my journey; you who had watched over my cradle and, as it were, the nest of my studies, again in the same place supported my first attempts when I made bold to fly; even when I had set sail during your absence and without having told you of my departure, although somewhat annoyed because I had not disclosed the matter to you, as I was wont to do, yet without ever accusing me of obstinacy, you remained firm in your friendship; nor before your eyes were your children abandoned by their teacher any more than were our motive and integrity questioned by you.[7]

4. Finally, you have brought about, you have stimulated, you have made possible whatever joy I am now experiencing in my life of leisure, the fact that I have escaped from the chains of superfluous desires, that I am now breathing again, am coming to myself, am recovering my senses after casting aside the burdens of fleeting cares, that I am earnestly seeking truth, that I am already on the road to find it, that I am hoping I shall arrive at it in the highest measure. But of what you have been the minister I have up till now grasped more by faith than I have comprehended by reason. For when I, in person, had made known to you the interior troubles of my soul, and time and again had stated emphatically that no condition of life seemed favorable unless it offered leisure for pursuing philosophy, and no life seemed happy unless it was devoted to philosophy, but that I was held back from enjoying such a life because of the burden of my duties on which I depended for a living and by many needs caused either by human respect or by the unreasonable distress of my friends, you were inspired with such great joy, you were kindled with such a holy enthusiasm for this kind of a life, that you said that, if by some means you could only

---

[7] These various autobiographical incidents and Augustine's obligation of gratitude to Romanianus are recounted in *Confessiones* II, iii, 5; III, i, 1; IV, vii, 12; V, viii, 14.

be free from the chains of those troublesome litigations, you would burst my fetters by sharing with me even your patrimony.[8]

5. And so, when you departed after furnishing us with the tinder, we never ceased longing for philosophy and for that life which was so pleasing to us, and it seemed fitting to think of nothing else. And we discussed it persistently but with less ardor; nevertheless we thought of it sufficiently to influence us. And since that flame was not yet at hand which was completely to overpower us, we regarded that desire with which we were inflamed as very intense, when behold! certain books of yours, packed with thought,[9] as Celsinus says, after exhaling upon us the fragrant incense of Arabia, after pouring upon that little flame a few drops of most precious ointment, enkindled in me an intense fire, Romanianus, a conflagration which surpassed anything you believed possible in me—what more shall I say—one which seemed incredible even to myself. What title of honor, what retinue of men, what empty desire of renown, finally, what enticement binding one to this mortal life then had any effect on me? Indeed, I completely and hastily returned to myself. But I looked back, I confess, from a long journey, so to speak, upon that religion which had been instilled into us in our childhood and which had been implanted within our very marrow; and yet, it was drawing me to itself without my being aware of it. And so, while wavering and hastening and hesitating, I seized the writings of Paul, the Apostle. For they surely would never have had such power, they never would have lived on, as it is clear that they have, if their words and doctrines were opposed to so great a good. I read the entire book most attentively and reverently.[10]

6. Then, indeed, when a faint light had been shed upon my path, the beauty of philosophy appeared to me in such a realistic manner that I should not speak of it to you who have always been inflamed with a desire for it even though you are not familiar with it; but if I had been able to show it to your adversary by whom I know not whether you are more annoyed than hindered, casting aside and abandoning Baiae,[11] delightful sub-

---

[8] In the *Confessiones*, VI, xiv, 24, Augustine discusses the plan formulated by himself and his friends to abandon the pleasures and business of the world and lead the life of recluses. He also speaks of the material aid offered by Romanianus for the execution of this design.

[9] Probably the *Enneads* of Plotinus. Cf. *De beata vita*, I, i, 4; *Confessiones*, VII, ix, 13; *De civitate Dei*, VIII, 11.

[10] This experience so graphically described seems to indicate that at this time faith and reason were closely associated in the mind of Augustine. The powerful influence exerted on him by the books 'filled with thought' [*libri quidam pleni*] and his comparison of them with the writings of St. Paul, would lead us to believe that the former assisted him in understanding more clearly what hitherto he had accepted on the evidence guaranteed by faith. A similar vivid experience is recorded in *De beata vita*, I, i, 4.

[11] A town on the Bay of Naples. The Romans erected many palatial buildings at Baiae.

urban gardens, dainty and sumptuous banquets, native actors and, finally, whatever inclinations he might have for any kind of pleasures whatsoever, as a fond and devoted lover, he would, indeed, hasten toward the beauty of philosophy, filled with admiration, desire, and burning love for it. For he has, it must be admitted, a certain nobility of soul or rather, as it were, the seed of nobleness which, while striving to blossom into true beauty, puts forth its misshapen and distorted leaves amid the scurvy of vices and the thickets of false opinions; and yet it does not cease to come into leaf and to become visible in so far as it is permitted, since only a few look carefully and with discernment into the dense shrubbery. From this source may be traced that kind thoughtfulness, the many evidences of refinement at banquets, that good taste, that charm, that chaste beauty in regard to all things, and that pleasing attractiveness which is diffused on all sides.

7.   This quality is commonly called philocalia. Do not despise this name because of the meaning usually ascribed to it. For philocalia and philosophy have been named as though they almost belonged to the same family and they wish to appear as in a single line of descent, so to speak, and they actually are. For what is philosophy? Love of wisdom. What is philocalia? Is it not love of beauty?[12] Ask this question of the Greeks. What, then, is wisdom? Is it not true beauty? Therefore, they are truly sisters born of the same parent; but the former, brought down from her place in heaven by the attraction of wanton desire, and enclosed within an ordinary cave, still retained the likeness in name to remind the fowler not to despise her. So her sister, while flying about freely, often recognizes her although she is unkempt, deprived of her wings, and greatly in need; but philosophy does not often set her free. For philocalia does not perceive to what family she really belongs unless philosophy makes it known. Licentius will give you a more pleasing interpretation of this whole fable—I have suddenly become an Aesop—in a poem, for he is almost a perfect poet. For with what great pleasure would he bury himself in the bosom of philosophy if only he were able with clear and unimpaired vision to behold true beauty, since he is already a lover of that which is false? How would he embrace you there after having recognized you as a true brother? You wonder at my words and perhaps you even smile at them. What if I should explain them to you as I have been wanting to do? What if at least the voice of philosophy herself could be heard, even if up to the present time her beautiful form could not be seen by you? You would, indeed, wonder at her but you would not ridicule her, you would not be without hope; take my word for it, you ought not give up hope in regard to anything but

---

[12] Augustine seems to have been familiar with Plato's *Symposium*. The subject of Augustine's erudition and of the sources from which he derived his knowledge of Platonism is treated in Nourrisson, *La philosophie de saint Augustin* (Paris: Didier et Cie, 1865), II, 89-146.

least of all in regard to such matters as you now despair of. There are instances of this everywhere. This kind of birds easily makes her escape, easily flies back, while many who greatly wonder at her are hindered from doing so.

8. But, to return to ourselves, Romanianus, let us, I say, become devoted to philosophy. In order that I may repay you somewhat, your son has begun to study philosophy. I am curbing him in its pursuit, that he may become more firm and steadfast after having first been equipped with necessary training. Do not fear that you are wanting in the necessary preparation; if I know you well, I merely desire favorable breezes for you. For what shall I say about your natural ability? Would that it were not as infrequent in other men as it is constant in you! There remain two faults and impediments in finding truth, but I do not fear them much in your case; and yet I fear that you may think little of yourself and despair of your finding it, or at least that you may believe you have found it. If your difficulty is of the kind first mentioned, perhaps an argument will remove it. For you have quite frequently been angry with the Academicians, the more grievously, indeed, the less familiar you were with their doctrines; the more willingly, because of the fact that you were always allured by the love of truth. So under your patronage I shall now hold a dispute with Alypius and I shall now easily convince you as to what I wish, at least I probably shall; for you will not see truth itself unless you devote yourself entirely to the study of philosophy. In regard to the other difficulty, however, the fact that you are perhaps assuming that you have found truth, even though you departed from us in an inquiring and hesitating mood, still, if any superstitious fear has returned to your mind, it will surely be rejected, either when I send you some of a discussion which we held concerning conscientious scruples (religione) or when I talk the matter over with you at length in person.

9. For at the present time I am doing nothing else but cleansing myself from vain and pernicious ideas. And so I do not doubt that it is better with me than it is with you. There is only one point on which I envy your good fortune, the fact that you alone are enjoying my Lucilianus. Or do you envy me because I said "my"? But what else did I say except yours and that of all of us who are one? And yet, why should I ask your assistance in my longing for him? Or am I at all worthy of your help? You merely know that you are indebted to him. But now I say to both of you: be on your guard lest you think you know anything except what you have learned in such a way, as that one, two, three, and four added together make the sum of ten; but beware also lest you think either that you will not learn truth by means of philosophy, or that truth can by no means be learned in this way. For take my advice or rather His, Who said, "Seek and you

shall find,"[13] that knowledge should not be despaired of and that it will be clearer than those very numbers. And now let us come to the subject of our discussion. For at least I have begun to fear that this introduction was exceeding the proper limit and that is not an unimportant matter. For, without doubt, moderation is divine but it will deceive us while leading us pleasantly along. I shall be more on my guard when I become wise.

IV. 10. After our former discussion which we condensed into the first book, we discontinued our argument for almost seven days, since we were reviewing the second, third, and fourth books of Vergil and as they seemed to be closely connected in time,[14] we busied ourselves with them. But while we were engaged in this work, Licentius became so interested in studying the art of poetry, that I felt obliged to restrain him somewhat. For he was unwilling to be called away from this occupation to any other task. But, finally, when I praised the excellence of philosophy for the purpose of resuming the discussion we had started about the Academicians, he not unwillingly assented. And by chance the day was so bright that it seemed particularly fitted to enlighten our minds. So we rose earlier than usual and performed whatever duties circumstances demanded in our country home. Then Alypius said: 'Before listening to your argument about the Academicians, I wish you would read for me the discussion which you say was completed during my absence; for, otherwise, I may either make a mistake or certainly experience great difficulty in following you, when the occasion arises for making a decision upon it. When this had been done and we noticed that almost the entire forenoon had been spent, we decided to return home from the field in which we had been taking a walk. And Licentius said: 'I should like to ask you, if it is not too much trouble, briefly to explain to me before dinner the entire doctrine of the Academicians, so that nothing in their teachings which might be of advantage to me may escape my notice.' 'I shall do this,' I replied, 'all the more willingly for this reason, that you will not eat much while you are thinking over this subject.' 'Do not be too sure of that,' he answered, 'for I have often noticed in regard to many people and especially my father, that he eats more heartily, the more absorbed he is in his cares. Then you also have observed that this was not the case with me when I was thinking about those metres, that I am always free from care during my meals. In fact, I am sometimes accustomed to wonder at this myself; for how can one account for the fact that we are seeking one thing with great persistency while we are thinking of something else? Or who is it, that becomes master of us when we are busied with both hands and teeth?' 'Listen, rather,' I said, 'to what you

---

[13] *Matthew*, VII, 7.
[14] Augustine probably refers to the unity of subject matter in these three books. They all treat of Aeneas' experiences at the court of Queen Dido.

have asked me about the Academicians lest I permit you to be pondering over those poetic forms, not only at banquets which have nothing to do with metre, but even at our disputations. If I, for my part, omit anything, Alypius is here to help me.' 'There is need of sincerity on your part,' said Alypsius; 'for if I ought to fear that you will conceal something, I think it would be difficult to entrap him from whom everyone who is acquainted with me knows that I learned those doctrines, especially since in disclosing the truth you will surely not be aiming at a victory rather than a sincere exposition of your thoughts.'

V.   11. 'I shall discuss the subject honestly,' I said, 'as you rightly prescribe. The Academicians are of the opinion that knowledge cannot be attained by man in so far as those things are concerned which pertain to philosophy—for Carneades said he did not care about other matters—and yet that man can be wise and that the whole duty of a wise man is accomplished in seeking truth, a statement which was also made by you, Licentius, in your argument; the conclusion is that the wise man should not assent to anything; for the fact that it is wrong for a wise man to assent to things that are uncertain, makes it necessary that he be in error. And they not only said that everything is uncertain but they even supported their statement by very forceful arguments. But they seemed to have appropriated the idea that truth cannot be grasped, from that definition of Zeno, the Stoic,[15] who said that that can be apprehended as true which has been so deeply impressed upon the mind from the source from which it came, that it could not proceed from that from which it did not come.[16] To express it more briefly and clearly, truth can be grasped by those signs which whatever is false cannot have.[17] They emphasized this precisely in order to prove conclusively that it cannot be found.[18] From this source have arisen the dissensions of philosophers, the unreliability of the senses, vain imaginations and frenzies, sophistical syllogisms and sorites in defense of that cause.[19] And since they had learned from this same Zeno, that

---

[15] Zeno of Citium, founder of the Stoic School of Philosophy.

[16] Augustine's knowledge of Zeno's doctrine of apprehension was probably derived from Cicero who treats of it in *Academica*, II, xviii, 57; II, xlviii, 148.

[17] According to Zeno a true impression is attained when the mind "seizes upon" an object in such a way that it is rightly apprehended. The result is an irresistible conviction in the mind of the perceiver, which is the only criterion of truth. Cf. *Academica*, I, xi, 41; II, x, 30-31. A clear explanation of Zeno's doctrine of assent and criterion of truth is given in E. Bevan, *Stoics and Sceptics* (Oxford: Clarendon Press, 1913), pp. 35-40; also in Sextus Empiricus, *Adversus mathematicos*, VII, 257.

[18] Cf. Cicero, *Academica*, II, xlvii, 145: 'Negat enim vos Zeno, negat Antiochus scire quicquam.'

[19] Cf. *Academica*, II, xlviii, 147, in which Cicero speaks of 'the aberrations of so many philosophers who are so vastly at discord concerning good things and their opposites, that the overthrow of so many and so famous schools is inevitable, since there can be but one truth and no more.'

nothing is more disgraceful than to conjecture, they very cleverly inferred that if nothing can actually be known and if it is disgraceful to express an opinion, then the wise man should never approve of anything.[20]

12. From this cause great odium was excited against them; for the logical consequence seemed to be that he who would not assent to anything would not accomplish anything.[21] Hence the Academicians seemed to portray your wise man as always sleeping and neglecting all his duties since they thought he never gave assent to anything. Hereupon, by introducing a kind of probability which they even mentioned as being similar to truth, they maintained that the wise man was in no way negligent in his duties since he had that which he was striving for; truth, however, lay hidden, being either crushed or obscured because of the darkness of our nature or the similarity existing in all things, although they said that the very withholding and, as it were, suspension of assent was, indeed, the great achievemen of the wise man. I think I have explained the whole matter briefly as you desired, and I have not departed from your injunction, Alypius, that is, I have discussed the subject as they say, *bona fide.* If I did not represent anything as it really is, or if I failed to mention something, it was not deliberate on my part. For honesty depends on the intention of the mind. For it seems that a man who has been deceived ought to be instructed, but a deceitful man ought to be avoided; the former needs a good teacher; the latter, a cautious pupil.

13. Then Alypius said: 'I am grateful to you since you have satisfied Licentius and have relieved me of the burden which was placed upon me. For you did not have to fear saying too little on the pretext of testing me— for how could it be done in another way?—more than I should have to fear if it were necessary for you to hand over the discussion to me in regard to any point. Therefore you will grant us the favor of not being loath to explain something that is still wanting, not so much to the question, as to a person questioning the difference between the New and the Old Academy.' I said, 'I confess, indeed, that I am loath to do so. Therefore you will grant us a favor—for I cannot deny that what you mention is an important point relative to the subject—if you will distinguish between those terms and explain the doctrine of the New Academy, while I take a little rest.' He replied, 'I should be tempted to believe that you wished to divert me from my dinner, if I did not rather think you were deterred from doing so by Licentius a little while ago and if his request had not demanded that an

---

[20] Cicero expresses approval of the Stoic doctrine of suspension of assent. Cf. *Academica,* II, xviii, 59: 'Si enim percipi nihil potest . . . tollendus adsensus est. Quid enim est tam futile quam quicquam approbare non cognitum?'
[21] Cf. *Academica,* II, xii, 39: '. . . qui aut visum aut adsensum tollit, is omnem actionem tollit e vita.' Also *Ibid.,* II, xix, 62: 'Sublata enim adsensione omnem et motum animorum et actionem rerum sustulerunt.'

[39]

involved question such as this, should be explained to him before dinner.' And while he was attempting to go on with the subject, my mother—for we were now at home—began to urge us to come to lunch, so that he had no opportunity to continue.

VI. 14. Then, after we had eaten enough to satisfy our hunger, Alypius said, as we were walking back toward the meadow: 'I should comply with your request, nor would I dare to refuse. For if nothing escapes me, I shall rejoice not only in your teaching but also in my memory. But if, perchance, I shall make a mistake on any point, you will rectify it so I shall not have to fear in regard to the due arrangement of the various steps. I think that the dissension of the New Academy was raised not so much against the old concept as against the Stoics.[22] For, truly, a dissension would not have to be thought of if the new question raised by Zeno did not have to be broken down and refuted. For the opinion about not perceiving, although agitated without any conflicts, yet even while engaging the attention of the older Academicians, was not regarded so abusively. It is easy to prove this even by the authority of such men as Socrates, Plato, and the rest of the older philosophers, who believed that they could be protected from error up to this point, that they did not rashly venture to give assent, although they did not introduce into their schools any special argument on this subject nor did they at any time distinctly inquire whether or not truth can be known.[23] But when Zeno had brought up this bold and new argument and maintained that nothing could be perceived unless it was so true that it was distinguished from the false by differentiating notes and that a conjecture ought not enter the mind of a wise man, and when Arcesilaus heard this, he denied that anything of this nature could be acquired by man and stated that the life of a wise man should not be intrusted to the shipwreck of conjecture. Whence he even concluded that one should not give assent to anything.[24]

15. But when the condition of affairs was such that the Old Academy seemed strengthened rather than attacked, Antiochus, the pupil of Philo, put in his appearance who, as it seemed to some, being more eager for his own renown than for truth, caused a dissension between the tenets of both Academies. For he said that the exponents of the New Academy were attempting to introduce something unusual and very far removed from the doctrine of the Old Academicians. In treating this matter he appealed to the authority of the old physicists and of other great philosophers, attacking even those very Academicians who maintained that they were striving after a resemblance of truth since they admitted they did not know truth

---

[22] Cf. Cicero, *Academica*, I, xii, 43-46.
[23] *Ibid.*, I, xii, 45.
[24] *Ibid.*, I, xii, 44-45; II, vi, 16.

itself; and he assembled many arguments which I think should be passed over now, and yet he defended nothing more than that the wise man can acquire a mental impression of things. This, I think, was the controversy between the New and Old Academicians.[25] If it is not correct, I shall request you to give Licentius accurate information in regard to both Academies. But if it is as I was able to express it, continue the argument which you began.'

16. Then I said: 'Licentius, how long are you going to take a rest in this discussion of ours which is more protracted than I anticipated? Have you heard who your Academicians are?' But smiling rather bashfully and somewhat disturbed by this reprimand, he replied: 'I regret that I so emphatically supported the statement, in opposition to Trygetius, that a happy life consists in the search for truth. For that subject agitates me to such a degree that I can only with difficulty not be unhappy, as I certainly seem worthy of sympathy in your estimation if you have any spirit of human kindness. But why am I so foolish as to torture myself? Or why do I fear when I am supported by so excellent a motive? Indeed, I shall not yield except to truth.' 'Are you in favor of the New Academicians?' I said. 'Very much,' he replied. 'Then, does it seem to you that they are speaking the truth?' I said. Then, when he was just about to express his agreement with them, becoming more cautious on account of the laughter of Alypius, he hesitated for some time and then said: 'Repeat that little question.' I said: 'Do you think that the Academicians are telling the truth?' And when he had again been silent for a long time, he answered: 'I don't know whether it is true; but still it is probable. For I see nothing more which I may strive after.' 'Do you know,' I said, 'that what is probable is said by them to be also like the truth?'[26] 'It seems so,' he replied. 'Then,' I said, 'the teaching of the Academicians is like the truth.' 'I believe so,' he answered. I said, 'Consider it more carefully, I entreat you. If anyone should say that your brother is like your father, and he did not even know your father, would he not seen foolish in your estimation?' And here he was silent for a long time; then he replied: 'This does not appear absurd to me.'

17. When I had started to reply, he said: 'Wait a little while, I beg of you.' And afterwards he said, smiling, 'Tell me, I ask you, are you now sure of your victory?' Then I said, 'Grant that I am sure; and yet you ought not for that reason abandon your cause, especially since we have engaged in this disputation to train you and to give you an opportunity of stimulating your mind.' He replied: 'Have I ever read the Academicians or have I been instructed in so many doctrines with which you, who are

---

[25] In the *Academica*, I, iv, 17; I, xii, 46, we find a summary of the history of the Old and the New Academy, as given by Antiochus.
[26] In characterizing the doctrine of Carneades, Cicero uses the terms *probabile* and *veri simile* interchangeably. Cf. *Academica*, II, x, 32.

well informed, are now approaching me?' I said: 'They by whom that doctrine was first defended never read the works of the Academicians. If, however, you lack training and ample instruction, your mental power ought not even for that reason be so weak that you should yield to my few words and questions without making any attack upon them. For I am now beginning to fear that Alypius is getting results with you more quickly than I desire; I shall not feel so secure when I go walking with him as an adversary.' 'Oh that I may soon be defeated then,' he said, 'so that I may listen to you some time while you discuss the subject and, what is more, that I may behold a spectacle than which nothing more enjoyable could be displayed. For since it pleased you to pour out (fundere) your arguments rather than to make full use (effundere) of them, if indeed you receive them in writing as they issue from your mouth and do not permit them to fall to the ground, so to speak, it will also be permitted you to read them; but somehow, when those very persons by whom an argument is killed appear before your very eyes,[27] a good disputation imbues the mind, if not more advantageously, certainly with greater enjoyment.

18. 'We are grateful to you,' I said; 'but those sudden joys of yours have forced you incidentally to sway from that subject than which you said no more enjoyable spectacle could be displayed. For if you see your father, than whom no one will drink in philosophy with more avidity after such a long thirst, investigating and discussing those questions with us—when that moment arrives I shall never consider myself more fortunate—what will it be fitting for you to think and to say?' At this point he began to weep and, when he was able to speak, extending his hands toward the heavens and looking upward, he said: 'When, O God, shall I see this? And yet I should not despair of receiving anything from You.' And when the attention of almost everyone of us had been diverted from the argument on account of our tears, after struggling with myself and with difficulty regaining my self-control, I said: 'Come now, and return to those forces of yours which I advised you some time ago to bring together so that you could be the future patron of the Academy, for surely I do not think that 'fear should overpower your limbs even before the sound of the trumpet'[28] or that you should desire to be taken captive so quickly from the desire of beholding others engaged in battle.' Then Trygetius, after observing that we had now regained our composure, said: 'Why should such a holy person as he not desire that God should grant him this favor before praying for it? Now, take my word for it, Licentius: for you who can find no reply to give and therefore desire to be overcome, seem to me to have little faith.' We all

27 Cf. Terence, *Heauton,* 242.
28 Vergil, *Aeneidos,* XI, 424.

laughed. Then Licentius said: 'You speak who are happy not in finding the truth, but certainly not in seeking it.'

19. When we became more cheerful on account of the gaiety of the youths, I said: 'Pay attention to the question and return to the subject with more determination and energy if you can.' 'Behold, I am ready in so far as I can be,' he said. 'For what if that person looking at my brother, should have found out by hearsay that he is like my father, can he be foolish or bereft of reason if he believes it?' 'Can he, at least, be called stupid?' I said. 'Not necessarily,' he replied, 'if he has not maintained that he knows it. For if probability is the logical consequence of what frequent rumors have spread abroad, he cannot be accused of any rashness.' Then I said: 'Let us examine the case one point at a time and settle it as if we were eye-witnesses. Behold! let us suppose a certain man is present whom we shall describe. Your brother comes in from somewhere. Thereupon the man asks: 'Whose son is this boy?' The answer is given, 'He is the son of a certain Romanianus.' Then the man says, 'How much he resembles his father! How accurately rumor has reported this to me!' Then you or some-one else says, 'Do you know Romanianus, my good man?' He answers, 'No, I do not know him but still I think the boy resembles him.' Will anyone be able to keep from laughing?' 'Indeed not,' Licentius said. 'Then,' I said, 'you see what follows.' 'I have seen it for sometime,' he replied, 'but still I desire to hear your conclusion; for you ought to begin supporting him whom you have adopted.' 'What if I should not draw a conclusion?' I said. 'The very analogy proclaims aloud that your Academicians ought to be ridiculed, who say that they are striving in this life after what is like truth when they do not know what truth itself is.'

VIII. 20. Then Trygetius said: 'It seems to me that the caution of the Academicians is far different from the foolishness of the man whom you depicted for us. For it is by a process of reasoning that they attain what they say resembles truth, whereas that foolish man of yours relied upon hearsay than which nothing could be more worthless as an authority.' 'As if, indeed, he would not be more foolish if he should say, 'Indeed, I do not know his father at all nor have I ever been told how much the boy resembles him; but still it seems to me he looks like him',' I replied. 'Of course he would be more foolish,' Trygetius said, 'but to what purpose is that?' 'Because,' I answered, 'such are those who say, 'Indeed, we do not know truth, but this which we see is like that which we do not know.' 'They say it is probable,' he said. I replied, 'How can you say that? Do you deny that they say it resembles truth?' Then he said, 'I wanted to say it for this reason, in order to omit that word "resembles." For it seemed to me that rumor rushed wantonly into your discussion since the Academicians would not even believe human eyes, much less, indeed, a thousand rumors, as the poets fashion,[29] but still they believe strange sources of illumination. But what kind of a defender of the Academy am I, pray? Or do you envy my freedom from responsibility in this subject of inquiry? Behold, you have Alypius whose arrival, I trust, will afford us a rest and whom we think you have been fearing, and not without reason, for a long time.'

21. In the silence which ensued both of them looked at Alypius. Then he said: 'Indeed, I would like to have the ability to aid both parties in some measure, if your augury were not a source of fear to me. But if hope has not deceived me, I should easily get rid of this fear. For I am consoled at once by the fact that the assailant of the Academicians here in person, has undertaken the burden of Trygetius who was almost defeated, and now it is probable that he is the victor by your avowal. I fear rather that I cannot avoid negligence by abandoning my duty, and boldness by taking upon myself another one. For I do not think you have forgotten that the rôle of judge was assigned to me.' Hereupon Trygetius said: 'That was one duty, but this is another; therefore we request you to consider yourself as not holding a public position for awhile.' 'I should not refuse,' he answered 'lest, while desiring to avoid the snares of pride than which no vice is more grievous, I should fall into them if I should hold the office which you gave me longer than you permit me to.

IX. 22. Then, O worthy accuser of the Academicians, I should like you to explain to me your position, that is, in whose defense you are opposing them. For I fear that, while refuting the Academicians, you may desire to prove yourself an Academician.' I replied, 'You know well, I believe that there are two kinds of accusers. For if Cicero very modestly said that he was an accuser of Verres[30] in such a way that he was a defender of the Sicilians, on that account it is necessary that he who accuses someone should have another whom he may defend.' And he replied, 'Have you at least, anything on which your opinion will rest firmly supported?' 'It is easy,' I said, 'for me to answer this question, especially since it is not unexpected. I have already considered this whole problem, and time and again my mind has been occupied with it. Therefore, listen, Alypius, to what you already know very well, I think: I have no desire to hold this disputation for the sake of arguing. Let that be sufficient which we practised beforehand with those youths, when philosophy willingly, as it were, joked with us. Therefore let those childish fables be removed from us. We are now treating of our life, of our morals, of our soul which, while returning, as it were, to the realm of its own divine origin, anticipates, by comprehending the truth, that it will conquer the enmities of all fallacies and will triumph over immoderate desires and, by accepting self-control, so to speak

---

[29] Vergil, *Aeneidos,* IV, 181 ff.
[30] Cf. Cicero, *Verres,* II, iv, 82.

as its bride, will so reign as to return more securely into heaven.[31] You see what I am speaking of. And now let us remove from our midst all those 'arms which should be prepared by a keen man'.[32] I have always desired that we who have lived together for such a long time and who have enjoyed so many discussions with one another, should devise some topic from which a new conflict, so to speak, may arise, but because memory is an untrustworthy guardian of what has been thought out, I desired that what we have been considering, should be written down in order that those youths might learn to take notice of these arguments and might try to take part in them and follow them up.

23.   Do you not know that I have no certain argument that I know of up to the present but that I am prevented from investigating this subject by the arguments and disputations of the Academicians? For I do not know how they have fashioned in their minds a certain probability—not to give up using their word, as yet—because man is not able to find truth; for this reason I became dilatory and very much undecided and I did not dare to ask what was not permitted the keenest and most learned men to find. Therefore unless I persuade myself that truth can be found before they persuaded themselves that it can not, I shall not dare to ask the question nor have I anything to defend. And so let us put away that question if you please; let us rather discuss as intelligently as we can whether truth can be found. And for my part, I have many arguments already which I shall strive to adduce against the reasoning of the Academicians; there is no difference between their view point and mine except that it seems probable to them that truth cannot be found, whereas to me it is probable that truth can be found. For ignorance of the truth is either peculiar to me, if they devised that argument, or it is certainly common to both of us.'

X.   24.   Then Alypius said: 'Now I shall enter the discussion with a feeling of assurance; for I see that you will be not so much an accuser as a helper. And so, not to digress any further, let us, I pray, first take care that, during the discussion in which I seem to have succeeded those who yielded to you, we may not fall into a dispute over a word, which we have often admitted is a very disgraceful procedure according to your insinuation and the authority of Cicero.[33] For, if I am not mistaken, when Licentius said that he was pleased with the opinion of the Academicians in regard to probability, you subjoined, since he made this statement without hesitation, as to whether he knew that probability was also called by them a resemblance to truth. And I know well that the opinions of the Academicians are familiar to you, if indeed it is from you that I became familiar with them.

---

[31] The diction of this passage is decidedly Neo-Platonic. In the *Retractationes,* I, i, 3, Augustine clarifies his meaning. Cf. note 6 of Book II.
[32] Vergil, *Aeneidos,* VIII, 441.
[33] Cf. Cicero, *De oratore,* I, 47; also Augustine, *De civitate Dei,* IX, 5.

Since, as I said, their teachings are fixed in your mind, I do not know why you are striving after words.' 'Take my word for it,' I said, 'this dispute is important not from the view point of words, but from that of the realities themselves; for I do not think that they were men who did not know how to give accurate expression to their ideas, but it seems to me that they selected these words both in order to conceal their doctrine from those who are too slow to comprehend and to disclose it to the more watchful. I shall explain why and how it appears so to me, when I have first discussed what men think has been said by these enemies, as it were, of human knowledge. Therefore I am very glad that our conversation today has turned to this point so that it may be perfectly clear what we are striving to get at. For they seem to me to have been very serious and prudent men. But if there is anything that we shall now argue, it will be against those who have believed that the Academicians were opposed to finding the truth.[34] And, lest you think that I am afraid, I shall even be glad to take up arms against them themselves (the Academicians) if they have defended those doctrines which we have read in their books, not to conceal their meaning lest certain sacred principles of truth should be carelessly handed over by them to defiled and irreverent minds, but because they really believed them. I would do this today, if the approach of evening did not compel us to return home.' Our discussion that day continued up to this point.

XI.   25. On the following day, however, although the weather was just as mild and pleasant, still it was with difficulty that we were released from our household duties. For we spent a great part of the day in writing letters especially, and when scarcely two hours were left, we went to the meadow. The extraordinary brightness of the sky lured us and made us resolve not to let even the short time which remained go to waste. So when we came to the tree which was our usual stopping place, I said: 'Since we ought not attempt much of a discussion today, I should like you young men to recall how Alypius replied to the question which troubled you yesterday.' Then Licentius said, 'It is so brief that there is no difficulty in remembering it; moreover, you see how trivial it is. For he disapproved, I believe, of your bringing up a question in regard to words when the main point was evident.' And I said, 'Did you notice well what the point of contention is or how important it is?' 'I seem to know what it is,' he replied, 'but I ask you to explain it a little. For I have often heard you say that it is disgraceful for those who are arguing, to be retarded by a question of words when

---

[34] In a letter written to an intimate friend, Hermogenianus, shortly after the completion of the treatise *Contra Academicos,* Augustine expresses the same opinion in regard to the Academicians. They merely appeared to be 'enemies of human knowledge,' [*eis tanquam cognitionis humanae inimicis*], whereas, in reality, they were serious, prudent men who concealed their true doctrine on account of the necessity of the times. Cf. also *Confessiones,* V, x, 19. Later on Augustine seems to have abandoned this view. Cf. *Enchiridion,* VII, 20.

there is no contention at all in regard to the points which are being disputed. But this is rather subtle, so much so, that I ought to ask you to explain it.'

26. 'Listen, then,' I said, 'to what the point really is. The Academicians call that probable or resembling truth, which can incite us to consider it without our giving assent to it. I say, indeed, without giving assent, so that we may not believe that what we are considering is true, nor think that we really know it, but still that we may consider it; for example, if someone should ask us whether a bright sun will rise today because last night was so calm and clear, I suppose we should affirm that we do not know, but still we should say that it seemed so. The Academician says, 'Such is the nature of all those things which I thought should be called either probable or like the truth. If you wish to call them by any other name, I have no objection. For it is sufficient for me that you have now well understood what I am speaking of, that is, in regard to the objects to which I am giving these names. For it is not fitting that a wise man be a fabricator of words but an investigator of facts.'[35] Do you understand now how those ridiculous things about which I was vexing you, have been forced out of my hands?' When both had replied that they understood and when they showed by the expression on their faces that they were requesting an answer from me, I said: 'What, do you think that Cicero, whose words I have just quoted, was so weak in using the Latin language that he gave unsuitable names to things of which he was treating?'

XII. 27. Then Trygetius said: 'Now, since we understand the condition of affairs, we do not wish to bring up any tricks in regard to words. Therefore, see rather what reply you would make to him who has come to our rescue against those upon whom you are attempting to rush again, as you have been urged to do.' And Licentius said: 'Wait, I beg of you; for it is dawning upon me, that I see that so great an argument should not so easily be snatched from you.' And after being absorbed in thought for some time, he said, 'Indeed, nothing seems more absurd to me than for anyone to say he is striving after the likeness of truth, who does not know what truth is; that word likeness which you mentioned does not bother me. For if I were asked whether there would be no rain tomorrow on account of the appearance of the sky, I would certainly reply that it is likely, since I do not deny that I know some things that are true. For I surely know that this tree cannot be made of silver, and I am not rash in affirming that I truly know many such things which I mention as being like the truth because I see that they are like it. Indeed, as for you, Carneades or some other Greek nuisance—to spare those of our own nation—why should I

---

[35] Cicero, *Academica,* fragment 19.

[47]

hesitate to go over to his side to whom I am bound as a prisoner by the right of victory? As for you, since you say that you do not know the truth, on what basis do you strive after this likeness of truth? For I could not give another name to it. Why then should we argue with him who is not able to speak?'

28. 'I should not fear deserters,' said Alypius. 'How much less should that Carneades against whom you who have been influenced, I know not whether by youthful or childish fickleness, thought that abusive language has easily been sufficient to strengthen against you his opinion which was always established as far as probability, the fact that we are so far removed from finding the truth, that you can furnish a great argument in your own case, since you were so changed in your opinion by one brief argument, that you really did not know what stand you ought to take. But let us postpone this point till some other time and also the knowledge which you admitted was impressed upon you in regard to this tree. For although you have now selected other subjects, still you ought to be carefully instructed in regard to what I said a little while ago. I believe, we had not yet proceeded to the question as to whether truth can be found, but I thought that important point should be set down at the very beginning of my defense, at which I noticed that you were already exhausted and overthrown, namely, whether the likeness of truth or probability, or any other name by which it can be called, which the Academicians say is sufficient for them, ought not be sought. If it seems to you that you are already a very good finder of truth, it is nothing to me. Afterwards, if you will not be ungrateful for my patronage, you will, perhaps, teach me those same things.'

XIII. 29. At this point, since through bashfulness Licentius feared the attack of Alypius, I said: 'You preferred to say everything, Alypius, rather than how to speak.' And he replied: 'Since this has long been known not only to me but to all of us, and since now, by your profession, you give sufficient evidence that you are skillful at speaking, I should wish that you would first explain the advantage of this inquiry of his which, I believe, is unnecessary and which it would be much more unnecessary for me to answer; or, if it should seem advantageous to you and if it cannot be explained by me, then I would entreat you not to refuse the duty of teacher.' I replied: 'You remember that I promised yesterday to treat of those names later on, but now the sun advises me to put back into their caskets those ludicrous treasures which I brought out for the boys, especially since I am displaying them now for the purpose of showing them off rather than of selling them. Now, before the darkness, which is wont to be the protector of the Academicians, lays hold of our pen, I desire that we all resolve to rise early tomorrow in order to disentangle this argument. So tell me, I ask you, whether you think that the Academicians had a fixed opinion in regard to truth and were unwilling to hand it over rashly to minds that were ignorant or not fitted for it, or that they really thought as their arguments would lead us to conclude.'

30. Then Alypius said: 'I shall not be so rash as to assert what was in their mind. In so far as may be ascertained from books, you know better the words by which they are accustomed to express their doctrine; but if you ask me what I think, I am of the opinion that truth has not yet been found. I also add that I think what you were demanding of the Academicians cannot be found, not only because of my personal opinion which you have often noticed, but also on the authority of great and eminent philosophers before whom either our weakness or their keenness of mind has somehow compelled us to bow and beyond whose authority nothing can be found in which to place our confidence.' 'This is what I desired,' I said. 'For I was afraid that, since both you and I seemed to have the same opinion on this question, our argument would remain unfinished, if no one appeared who, by taking up the other side, would force the issue to be brought to the point so that it would be discussed carefully in so far as we are able. So, if this had been the result, I was prepared to ask you to assume the rôle of the Academicians just as if it seemed to you that they not only argued, but even thought that truth can not be understood. Therefore the subject of debate between us now is whether it is probable, according to their arguments, that nothing can be known and that assent ought not be given to anything. If you carry your point, I shall willingly yield; if, however, I shall be able to show you that it is much more probable that a wise man is able to arrive at the truth and that assent need not always be withheld, you will have no reason, I believe, for not permitting yourself to embrace my opinion.' Since this was agreeable to him and to those who were present, we returned home, as it was now twilight.

I. 1. On the day following the discussion comprising the second book, when we had assembled in the Baths—for the weather was too unpleasant for us to go down to the meadow—I began the conversation as follows: 'I think you are now familiar with the subject which we decided to investigate. But before undertaking my part, which is to give an explanation of the subject, I ask you to be willing to listen to a few words about our hope, our life, our moral nature—words not unsuited to the topic under discussion. Our concern, I believe, is not insignificant or of little value, but indispensable and of the greatest importance, namely, to seek the truth with great earnestness.[1] This has been agreed upon between Alypius and me. For the other philosophers have thought that their wise man has found the truth, and the Academicians have declared that their wise man ought to make every possible effort to find it and that he persistently continues this attempt. But, since truth either lies hidden or appears only in an obscure manner, in order to regulate his life, he strives after what is probable and what resembles truth. This point also was treated in your discussion yesterday. For since the one affirmed that man is made happy by finding truth, and the other, merely by a diligent search for truth, none of us doubt that we ought to consider any affair of more importance than this. Then, does it seem to you that we took this view of the case yesterday? You were even permitted to devote yourselves to your studies. For you, Trygetius, passed the time pleasantly at the poems of Vergil, and Licentius occupied himself with composing verses; so smitten was he with love for this occupation that I thought I ought to bring up this discussion for his sake especially, so that in his estimation philosophy might lay claim to and appropriate a greater share of his attention—for it is now time that it should —than either poetry, or any other kind of instruction.

II. 2. But I ask you, did you not pity us because, although we had gone to bed the night before with no other thought in mind than to rise for the continuation of our discussion which had been postponed, so many things regarding our household came up, which had to be taken care of, that we became absorbed in these and were able to devote scarcely the two last hours of the day to ourselves. Therefore it has always been my opinion

---

[1] Augustine's passion for truth was one of his outstanding characteristics. The *Contra Academicos* is the first treatise mentioned in the *Retractationes,* the general review of his literary output, written by Augustine toward the close of his life. In this work he speaks with subtle approval of having devoted his first literary efforts to the important task of proving that certitude is possible of attainment: '. . . nondum baptizatus, contra Academicos vel de Academicis primum scripsi, ut argumenta eorum, quae multis ingerunt veri inveniendi desperationem, et prohibent cuiquam rei assentiri, et omnino aliquid, tanquam manifestum certumque sit, approbare sapientem, cum eis omnia videantur obscura et incerta, ab animo meo, quia et me movebant, quantis possem rationibus amoverem.' Cf. *Retractationes,* I, i, 1.

that nothing is necessary for a man who is already wise; but in order that he may become wise, fortune is very necessary, unless it appears otherwise to Alypius.' Then Alypius replied: 'I do not know as yet how much right you attribute to fortune. For if you think that fortune itself is necessary for despising fortune, I am also of the same opinion. But if you grant nothing else to fortune except those things which cannot supply the needs of the body unless fortune is favorable, I do not agree with you. For either it is permitted, when fortune is adverse and unfavorable, that a man who is not yet wise but still is desirous of wisdom, make use of those things which we admit are necessary for life, or it must be granted that fortune rules even in the life of every wise man, since the wise man himself cannot fail to be in need of those things which are necessary to sustain the body.'

3. 'You say, then,' I replied, 'that fortune is necessary for the man who is striving after wisdom, but you deny that it is necessary for the wise man.' He said: 'It is not irrelevant to return to my exact statement. Therefore, I shall now also inquire of you whether you think fortune is of any assistance in despising itself. If you think this is so, then I say that the man who is eager for wisdom is greatly in need of fortune.' 'I think so,' I replied, 'if, indeed, he will be rendered such a service by fortune as will make him able to despise it. Nor is this absurd; for so, too, are the breasts (of our mothers) necessary for us when we are young since they make it possible for us to live and grow strong afterwards without them.' 'If my idea does not differ,' he said, 'I may harmonize our opinions, unless someone thinks the subject ought to be discussed, by saying that it is not the breasts themselves, nor fortune, but a certain other factor which makes us despisers of fortune or the breasts.' 'It is a simple matter to use another simile,' I said. 'For just as no one goes across the Aegean Sea without a boat, or some kind of a conveyance or, not to fear Daedalus[2] himself, without any means at all suitable for such an undertaking or without some more secret power, although he has in view nothing else than to arrive at his destination and, when he has attained his purpose, is prepared to cast aside and despise all those things which furnished him the means of accomplishing his end, so, too, whoever wishes to arrive at the harbor of philosophy and at a lasting and peaceful country, so to speak, must have fortune, it seems to me, to attain that which he has desired, since, to pass over other points, if he is blind or deaf, he cannot obtain what lies in the power of fortune to give him. When he has obtained this, although it may be thought that he lacks certain things which have reference to bodily health, still it is evident that those things are not necessary in order that he

---

[2] A mythical artist and inventor who, in order to escape from the Minotaur in the labyrinth on the island of Crete, fashioned wings of feathers and wax for himself and his son and flew across the Aegean Sea. According to the myth, his son, Icarus, fell into the sea but Daedalus succeeded in arriving at Sicily.

may be wise, but in order that he may live among men.' 'On the contrary,' he replied, 'if he should be blind and deaf, according to my way of thinking, he would despise the attaining of wisdom and would abhor life itself on account of which wisdom is sought.'

4. 'But still,' I said, 'since our very life, while we are living here, is in the power of fortune and since a man cannot become wise unless he is alive, must we not admit that its favor is necessary to conduct us to wisdom?' 'But since wisdom,' he replied, 'is not necessary except for the living and since no life is removed from the need of wisdom, I have no fear of fortune in prolonging my life. For I desire wisdom because I am living; I do not desire life because I am eager for wisdom. So if fortune should take away my life, it would remove the reason for my seeking wisdom. Therefore I do not see why, in order to become wise, I should either desire the favor of fortune or fear its disfavor, unless perhaps you mention other circumstances.' Then I said: 'You do not think, then, that he who is striving after wisdom is hindered by fortune from attaining wisdom even if fortune does not take away his life?' 'I do not think so,' he said.

III. 5. I replied: 'I wish you would tell me briefly what difference there is in your estimation between a wise man and a philosopher.' 'I think,' he said, 'that there is no difference between them except that in the case of him who is striving after wisdom, there is only the eagerness for those things for which there is a real disposition in the wise man.' 'What, pray, are those things?' I said; 'for it seems to me that there is no difference except that the one knows wisdom, the other desires to know it.' 'If you define knowledge within reasonable limits,' he answered, 'you have expressed the idea rather clearly.' 'No matter how I define it,' I said, 'everyone agreed that there cannot be knowledge of things that are false.' He replied: 'It seemed to me an objection should be raised against that statement lest by my thoughtless agreement your language should easily go riding along the fields of that original question.' 'It is quite evident,' I said, 'that you have left me no opportunity to go riding. For unless I am mistaken, we have arrived at the very goal which I have long been striving to reach. For if, as you astutely and truly said, there is no difference between the man who is striving after wisdom and the wise man except that the former loves, while the latter possesses the knowledge of wisdom—whence you did not even hesitate to express the very name itself, that is, a certain disposition [habitum]—but no one can have knowledge in his mind who has learned nothing, moreover he has learned nothing who knows nothing, and no one can know what is false, then the wise man knows truth since you have already admitted that he has the knowledge of wisdom in his mind, that is, a disposition for it.' He said: 'I do not know whether I would be guilty of boldness if I should wish to deny that I admitted that in a

[52]

wise man there is a disposition for seeking divine and human things. But I do not see why you should think there is not a disposition for finding probability.' 'Do you grant,' I said, 'that no one knows what is false?' 'I readily admit that,' he said. Then I said, 'Now, say, if you can, that the wise man does not know wisdom.' 'But why?' he replied; 'do you decide everything by this distinction that it cannot seem to him that he has comprehended wisdom?' 'Give me your right hand,' I said; 'for, if I remember, I said yesterday that I would accomplish what I am happy to say was just now not inferred by me, but presented to me by you of your own accord. For when I said that there was this difference between me and the Academicians, that it seemed probable to them that truth cannot be grasped, while to me it seems that I, indeed, have not yet found the truth but that it can be found by the wise man, just now, when you were hard pressed by my question whether the wise man does not know wisdom, you said it seems to him that he knows it.' 'What is the conclusion then?' he said. 'That, if it seems to him that he knows wisdom,' I said, 'it does not seem to him that the wise man can know nothing; or if wisdom is nothing, I wish you would admit it.'

6. 'I would really believe,' he said, 'that we have reached the end of our discussion, but suddenly, when you spoke about extending our right hands, I see clearly that we have digressed and wandered far from our subject because yesterday no other argument seemed to have been established by us except that, while you maintained, I denied that the wise man can attain the comprehension of truth; at present I am truly of the opinion that I made no concession to you except that it can seem to the wise man that he has acquired wisdom in regard to probable things; and yet I think none of us doubt that I placed this wisdom in the search for things human and divine.' 'You will not be extricated,' I said, 'merely by confusing ideas; for it seems to me you are arguing now just for your own practice, and since you know well that up to the present time these young men have scarcely been able to understand what is expressed with astuteness and subtlety, you are taking advantage, so to speak, of the want of knowledge of your judges in order that you may be permitted to say whatever you wish without anyone's contradicting you. For you said a little while ago when I asked whether the wise man knew wisdom, that it seemed to him that he knew it. Therefore he to whom it seems that the wise man knows wisdom surely does not think that the wise man knows nothing. For this cannot be maintained unless anyone would dare to say that wisdom is nothing. From this it follows that you and I are of the same opinion, for it seems to me that the wise man does not know nothing, and to you also, I believe, since you agree that it seems to the wise man that the wise man knows wisdom.' Then he said: 'I do not think I wish to practice cleverness

[53]

any more than you do and I am surprised at this; for you do not need any training of this type. For perhaps hitherto I have been intellectually blind in seeing a difference between 'it seems to him that he knows' and 'he knows' and between 'wisdom which has been placed in seeking truth' and 'truth.' I do not see how one of these two statements of ours can coincide with the other.' Then, since we were now being called to lunch, I said: 'I am not displeased because you are so vigorously opposing me; for either both of us do not know what we are talking about and should make an effort not to be so disgraceful, or one of us does not know, a fact which it is not less disgraceful to abandon and pass over. But this afternoon we shall mutually return to the question. For when it seemed to me that we had now reached the end, you still mixed blows with me.' Then as they all burst into laughter, we departed.

IV. 7. When we returned, we came upon Licentius longing for the verses to be devised, whom the Muse had never aided in his thirst for poetry. For almost in the middle of the lunch, although the beginning of our repast was the same as the end, he had stood up without attracting any attention and had not even taken a drink. I said to him: 'Indeed, I desire you to devote yourself occasionally to that art of poetry which you have so eagerly desired, not because attaining perfection in it seems to me of very much value, but because I see you are so fascinated by it that only with reluctance can you tear yourself away from it, a situation which usually happens after perfection has been acquired. Then, since you are so musically inclined, I should prefer to have you force your verses upon our ears than to have you sing words which you do not understand, as is customary in the Greek tragedies after the fashion of the little birds that we see shut up in cages. But still I advise you to continue your drinking, if you wish, and to return to our school, if indeed the *Hortensius* and philosophy deserve anything of you, whose delicious first fruits you have already tasted in that discussion of ours[3] which moved you more powerfully than did those poems to the knowledge of things which are important and really worth while. But while I desire to call you back to the circle of those kinds of knowledge which cultivate the mind, I fear that it may become a labyrinth for you, and I almost regret that I curbed you by force.' He blushed with embarrassment as he departed for a drink, for he was very thirsty, and the opportunity was given to avoid me as I was about to say perhaps more and harsher words.

8. Upon his return, since all were eagerly waiting, I began the discussion as follows: 'Is it so, Alypius, that you and I do not agree on a point which, it seems to me, is now very evident?' 'It is not strange,' he said, 'if

---

[3] *Nostro* as found in the *Editio Amerbachiana* seems to be preferable to *vestro*, the reading in the *Corpus scriptorum ecclesiasticorum Latinorum*.

what you say is clear to you, should be obscure to me, if indeed there are many obvious things which can be more obvious to some and likewise certain obscure matters which may be more obscure to others. For if this point is really clear to you, take my word for it, there is someone else to whom this idea which is evident to you, is still more clear, and there is likewise someone else to whom this point which is obscure to me is more obscure. But in order that you may not consider me stubborn any longer, I shall entreat you to make this clear idea more evident.' I replied, 'Listen carefully, I beg of you, and as if the trouble of making a reply had been dispelled for a while. For if I know both you and myself well, what I say will easily clarify the matter if we make an effort to do so, and one of us will quickly persuade the other. Did you say, then, or was I perhaps deaf, that it seems to the wise man that he knows wisdom?' He admitted that he said it. 'Let us not make any mention of that wise man for awhile,' I said. 'As for you yourself, are you wise or are you not?' 'By no means,' he replied. 'But still, I wish you would tell me,' I said, 'what you think about the wise Academician; does it seem to you that he knows wisdom?' 'Do you think,' he replied, 'that it seems to him he knows' or 'he knows' means the same thing or something different? For I fear that this confusion of terms may provide a safe retreat for someone of us.'

9. 'This is,' I said, 'that Etruscan contention of words, as it is wont to be called, when it is not an explanation of the question but an objection raised against it by someone else, that seems to provide a remedy for the argument which has not even been attacked. Even our poet—to attract the attention of Licentius for a little while—in his poem *Bucolics*[4] has aptly declared this to be boorish and uncultured, (namely), when one person asks the other where the breadth of the heavens does not extend further than three ells but the latter asks in reply: 'In what lands do flowers grow on which are written the names of kings?'[5] I entreat you, Alypius, not to think that this is permissible in our country house, and I also pray that these Baths may surely bear some recollection of having the honor of a place devoted to philosophical discussions. Now make a reply, if you please, to what I ask you: does it seem to you that the wise men of the Academicians know wisdom?' He replied, 'Not to go into details by weighing words against words, I think that it seems to him he knows it.' 'Then,' I said, 'does it seem to you that he does not know it? For I am not asking you what it seems to you the wise man thinks but whether you think that the wise man knows wisdom. You can, I believe, say either yes or no.' He said, 'Would that it were as easy for me as it is for you or that it were as difficult for you as it is for me; you would not be so exasperating nor would you

---

[4] Vergil, *Eclogues*, III, 105.
[5] *Ibid.*, III, 106 ff.

be expecting anything in these arguments. For when you asked me what I thought about the wise Academician, I answered that it seemed to me that he thought he knew wisdom, lest I should either be rash in asserting that I knew or be not less rash in saying that he knew.' I said: 'I ask you as a great favor, in the first place, to deign to answer what I ask you and not what you are safe in asking; secondly, to put aside for the time being my hope which I know is of no less concern to you than your own—it is certain that, if I am entrapped by my questioning, I shall quickly go over to your side and close the argument—finally, to banish that worry by which I see you are affected and to listen more attentively that you may easily know what reply I wish you to give me. For you said you did not say yes or no—which you certainly should do to the question I am asking—lest you should rashly say that you know what you do not know; as if, indeed, I asked what you really know and not what you think. Therefore, I shall now ask you the same question more simply—if it can be expressed more simply: does it or does it not seem to you that the wise man knows wisdom?' He replied, 'If a wise man such as reason makes known to us can be found, it seems to me he can know wisdom.' 'Reason, then,' I said, 'discloses to you that the wise man is he who is not ignorant of wisdom; and rightly so. For it would not be proper if it seemed otherwise to you.

10.   Therefore I now ask you whether a wise man can be found. For, if he can, he can also know wisdom and the whole argument between us has been settled. But if you say that he cannot, the question will not be raised as to whether the wise man knows anything, but whether anyone can be wise. After this has been determined, we shall have to withdraw from the Academicians, and carefully and assiduously discuss that question with you in so far as we are able. For they were of the opinion or rather it seemed to them, both that man can be wise and yet that knowledge cannot fall to the lot of man—for that reason they asserted that the wise man knows nothing—but it seems to you that he knows wisdom, which certainly does not mean that he knows nothing. For at the same time we were agreed, as were also the ancients and the Academicians themselves, that no one can know what is false;[6] whence it now remains that you either maintain that wisdom is nothing or that you admit that the wise man is portrayed by the Academicians as a person of whom reason will not admit and, putting aside these alternatives, that you agree we should ask whether man can

---

[6] In *Academica*, II, xxxii, 103, Cicero quotes from a book written to Lucilius, the poet, by Clitomachus, the successor of Carneades in the New Academy: 'id autem non esse satis cur alia posse percipi dicas, alia non posse, propterea quod multa falsi perceptum et cognitum possit esse.' Cf. also *Ibid.*, II, xiii, 40, in which Cicero thus describes the doctrine of the Academicians as expounded by Carneades: '. . . eorum, quae videntur, alia vera sunt, alia falsa, et quod falsum est, id percipi non potest: quod autem verum visum est id omne tale est, ut eiusdem modi falsum etiam possit videri.'

attain such wisdom as reason makes known. For we ought not nor can we rightly call any other kind wisdom.'

V. 11. 'Even if I should grant,' he said, 'what I see you are eagerly striving for, that the wise man can know wisdom and that we have grasped something that the wise man can apprehend, yet it appears to me that the entire claim of the Academicians has by no means been weakened. For I foresee that considerable opportunity has been reserved for their defense and that their argument for the suspension of assent has not been completely broken down, since they cannot fail their cause on this very ground on which you think that they have been guilty. For they will say in regard to the assertion that nothing is apprehended and that assent should not be given to anything, that even this point about not apprehending anything, which they had persuaded themselves as being probable throughout the entire span of life even including you, has now been extorted from them with this conclusion that, if at that time the force of this argument was invincible because of my mental slowness or precisely on account of its own inherent strength, they cannot be moved from their position since they can still boldly assert that not even now should assent be given to anything. For sometime, perhaps, something may be discovered by themselves or someone else against what is being so effectively and credibly said, and their likeness and some kind of a copy of them, so to speak, ought to be noted in the case of that well known Proteus[7] who, it is said, was wont to be seized when he was by no means being captured, and those who were searching for this same man never detected him unless a divine being of some kind informed them. Would that such a being were present and would vouchsafe to show us the truth about which we are so greatly concerned! I also shall admit that it is against their will that they (the Academicians) have been vanquished, a fact which I by no means consider likely.'

12. 'I am pleased,' I said; 'indeed, I did not desire anything further. For behold, I entreat you, how many and how great advantages have been given to me. The first is that the Academicians are already said to have been convicted in such a way that nothing now remains for their defense except the fact that it is impossible to defend them. For how is it possible for anyone to think or believe that he who has been vanquished should boast that he is victorious by that very argument by which he himself has been overcome? Secondly, if there is now any conflict with them, it is not due to the fact that they say nothing can be known but to the fact that they maintain that assent should not be given to anything. So we are now of the same opinion. For they likewise think as I do, that the wise man knows wisdom. But still they advise him that he ought to withhold his assent.

---

[7] Cf. Vergil, *Georgics*, IV, 388 ff.

For they merely say that it seems so to them but that they by no means know; just as if I should avow that I actually know it. I also say that such a thing seems to me to be true; for I am as foolish as they certainly are, if they do not know wisdom. But I think we ought to establish something, that is, the truth. I consult them on this very question, whether they deny, that is, whether they are of the opinion that one should not give his assent to truth. They will never make such a statement but they will maintain that truth cannot be found. Therefore they claim me in some measure an associate of theirs, since both of us do not disagree and therefore we must necessarily agree that assent should be given to truth. But, they say, who will point out the truth? I shall not care to dispute with them in regard to this; it is sufficient for me that it is improbable that the wise man knows nothing, lest they be forced to make the very absurd statement either that wisdom is nothing or that the wise man does not know wisdom.

VI.   13.   But you said, Alypius, that someone can show us the truth. I ought to strive earnestly not to disagree with him. For you said not only briefly but even reverently that only some divinity can show man what is true. Therefore I have heard nothing in this discussion of ours, that has given me greater pleasure, nothing that seems more important, nothing more likely, and, if this divine Being is present, as I trust He is, nothing that is more true. For that Proteus—with what great nobility of mind you referred to him, with what great allusion to the very best kind of philosophy!—in order that you young men may see that poets should not be entirely disregarded by philosophy, that Proteus just mentioned is represented as the likeness of truth. It is the character of truth, I say, which Proteus sustains and supports in poetry; and no one can attain it, if, deceived by false representations, he loosens or relaxes his hold on the knots of reason.[8] For they are those likenesses which try to deceive and mislead us, as material things are wont to do, through those senses which are necessary for this life, even when truth is held and, as it were, is grasped by our very hands.[9] Consequently, this third advantage which has been given to me is something which I cannot estimate at its full value. For my most intimate friend agrees with me, not only in regard to the probability of human life,

---

[8] In this passage we observe a trace of Augustine's doctrine of illumination which holds an important place in his theory of knowledge. Augustine seems to be of the opinion that the human mind can not of itself recognize truth. In order to express true judgments it requires direct assistance from God. Hence he experiences great pleasure at the wish expressed by Alypius, (III, iv, 11), that a divine Being were present in order to point out to them the truth about which they were so greatly concerned and which Proteus-like seemed unable to be grasped.

[9] According to Augustine there is an essential distinction between the intellectual knowledge of things which do not change and the reasoned knowledge of sensible things. The former alone, in his opinion, deserves the name of wisdom. Cf. *Soliloquia*, I, iii, 8; *De magistro*, XII, 29.

but also in regard to religion itself, which is the most evident indication of a true friend, if indeed friendship is correctly and accurately defined as 'the agreement with good will and affection in reference to human and divine matters.'[10]

VII. 14. But lest it should seem that the arguments of the Academicians are spreading about a sort of mist, or lest some people should think that we are so proud as to oppose the authority of very learned men among whom Cicero,[11] especially, cannot fail to influence us, if it is agreeable to you, I shall first say a few words against those whose arguments seem to be opposed to truth; then I shall show you, as I see it, what reason the Academicians had for concealing their opinion. And so, Alypius, although I see that you are in perfect agreement with me on this subject, nevertheless defend their cause for a little while and answer (the arguments I shall raise against them). He replied: 'Since you have proceeded today under such favorable auspices, as they say, I shall not prevent your having a complete victory and I shall attempt to uphold their views, since I am now more safe in that this duty is being imposed upon me by you; if, however, you should prefer to convert into an uninterrupted speech what you say you intend to treat of in this argument, if you consider it advantageous, do not let me, who am already your prisoner, be tortured as an obstinate adversary by those petty weapons—but you, in your kindness, have no such intention.'

15. And since I noticed that they were eager for the argument, I began as it were, another introduction: 'I shall comply with your wishes,' I said, 'and although I had anticipated after my strenuous labor in the school of rhetoric, that I would take a little rest in this light armor by directing the argument through asking questions rather than by taking part in the discussion, yet, since we are very few in number so that it is not necessary for me to talk in a way that may be injurious to my health and since for the same reason I have desired that this pen[12] be, so to speak, the charioteer and manager of our discussion, lest my mind should hasten along more rapidly than the well-being of my body demands, listen and I shall make known to you in an uninterrupted talk, as you desire, what I think about

---

[10] Cicero, *Laelius,* XX.
[11] In the *Academica,* II, iii, 8, Cicero speaks of himself as an Academician and supports the Academician doctrine of probability: 'Neque inter nos et eos, qui se scire arbitrantur, quidquam interest, nisi quod illi non dubitant, quin ea vera sint, quae defendunt: nos probabilia multa habemus, quae sequi facile, affirmare vix possumus.' Probability, in his opinion is sufficient for man as a guide of life. Cf. *Ibid.,* II, xxxi, 99: 'Quidquid acciderit specie probabile, si nihil se offeret, quod sit probabilitati illi contrarium, utetur eo sapiens: ac sic omnis ratio vitae gubernabitur. Etenim is quoque, qui a vobis sapiens ind citur, multa sequitur probabilia, non comprehensa, neque percepta, neque assensa, sed similia veri; quae nisi probet omnis vita tollatur.'
[12] Augustine here assigns ill-health as his reason for requesting that their discussions be taken down in writing.

this affair. But first let us see what the reason may be that the friends of the Academicians are wont to boast so extravagantly. For in the books of Cicero which were written in defense of this cause[13] there is a certain passage which I think is embellished with refined elegance, but which some consider strong and forcible. It certainly is difficult for anyone not to be influenced by what is said there:[14] 'Second place is given to the wise Academicians by all the members of other schools who think that they themselves are wise,[15] since it is necessary for everyone to claim first place for himself. From this circumstance it can probably follow that he is rightly first in his own judgment who is second in the opinion of all others.

16. Suppose, for example, that the wise Stoic is present; for the indignation of the Academicians has been aroused against those Stoics above all others. Therefore, if Zeno or Chrysippus[16] should be asked who is wise, he will reply that it is he whom he has described. On the other hand, Epicurus[17] or any other of the Stoics' opponents will deny this and will maintain that, in his opinion, the wise man is he who has had most experience in striving after pleasure.[18] Thence arises a dispute. Zeno and the entire Stoic School emphatically assert that man was made for nothing else but virtue,[19] that by its luster virtue attracts souls to itself without offering them any external advantages or any reward as an enticement, that the pleasure recommended by Epicurus is common only to beasts, and that it is wrong for any man and especially for the wise man to form a companionship with them. On the other hand, that Bacchus so to speak, summons a crowd of intoxicated men for his defense and yet of those who

---

13 *Academica priora* and *Academica posteriora.* Augustine always quotes from the latter.
14 The passage quoted by Augustine is a fragment from one of the lost books of the *Academica posteriora,* probably from the second book. The larger part of the first book has been preserved but only fragments of the remaining books are extant.
15 Cicero portrays each school of philosophy as postulating a *sapiens* who was depicted as a perfect representative of its own doctrines.
16 Chrysippus was born at Soli in Cilicia, in 280 B.C. He succeeded Cleanthes, the pupil of Zeno of Citium, as head of the Stoic School and under him it reached its full development. He has been regarded as the second founder of the school. Cicero discusses the doctrine of Chrysippus in *Academica,* II, xxvii, 87; II, xlv, 138; II, xlvi, 140; II, xlvii, 147.
17 Epicurus, the founder of the Epicurean School, was born at Samos about 340 B.C. For the history of Epicureanism our chief primary source is Lucretius, *De rerum natura.* Cicero, Plutarch, and Diogenes Laertius are the most important secondary sources. Cicero discusses the doctrine of Epicurus in *Academica,* I, ii, 5-6; II xxx, 97; I, ii, 6; I, vii, 27-28; II, xxv, 79-80; *De finibus bonorum et malorum,* I, 7; II, 7, 20, 30; *De natura deorum,* I, 16; I, 25.
18 In the *Academica,* I, ii, 7, Cicero represents Epicurus as declaring that he can not conceive of any good which is lacking in pleasures of sense: '. . . sine voluptatibus sensum moventibus.' This opinion of Epicurus is also referred to in *Tusculanae disputationes,* III, 47; *De finibus bonorum et malorum,* II, 7, 20, 30 Cicero admits, however, in the *De finibus,* II, 7, that this statement has many limitations.
19 The Stoic doctrine of virtue is discussed by Cicero in *Academica,* I, x, 36-38.

are in search for him whom, in their revels, they may tear to pieces with their sharp finger nails and with bespattered mouths, and while exalting the name of pleasure, its sweetness, its repose, with the people as his witnesses, he violently argues that he believes no one can be happy except by means of pleasure. If the Academician should happen to enter the dispute, he will hear both parties urging him to join their cause, but if he should yield to the one or the other, he will be proclaimed foolish, ignorant, and rash by those whom he abandons. And so, as he listens carefully, now to this side and now to that side, if his opinion is asked, he will say that he is in doubt. Now, ask the Stoic who is the better: the Epicurean who says that the Stoic is raving or the Academician who asserts that he must deliberate about so important a matter; no one doubts that the Academician will be preferred. Again, turn to the Epicurean and ask him whom he likes the better: Zeno by whom he is called a beast, or Arcesilaus[20] from whom he hears 'perhaps you are speaking the truth, but I shall investigate the matter more carefully.' Is it not evident that Epicurus will think that the entire Stoic School is mad but the Academicians in comparison with them are virtuous and discreet men?' And so in regard to almost all the schools Cicero very eloquently presents, as it were, a mirror most pleasing to his readers, showing, so to speak, that there is not one of them who, while giving first place to himself, as must needs happen, does not say that he awards second place to him who, he has noticed, does not oppose him but is in doubt. In this matter I[21] shall not contradict him nor shall I take any renown away from them.

VIII. 17. It may, indeed, appear to some that Cicero was not joking about this matter, but that he desired certain vain and worthless things to be inferred and to follow as a logical consequence, since he was opposed to the frivolity of those very Greeks. Certainly if I should wish to oppose this instability, what is there to prevent me from easily proving how much less an evil it is to be unlearned than to be unteachable? Hence it follows that, when that boastful Academician has offered himself as a pupil to each (of them) and no one has been able to persuade him that he thinks he knows, their hearty agreement afterwards becomes a source of ridicule. For now each one will declare openly that any other of his opponents has not learned anything but that the Academician, indeed, cannot learn anything. As a result, he will be cast out of the schools of all of them, not by ferules, which would be more disgraceful than annoying, but by the clubs

---

[20] The founder of the New Academy. He spent his life combating the Stoic doctrine of knowledge and maintained that all scientific knowledge is impossible. Cicero treats of the philosophic views of Arcesilaus in *Academica*, I, iv, 17; I, x, 35; I, xii, 44 ff.
[21] Augustine proceeds (viii, 17 ff.) to outline his own view of the history of philosophy.

and the cudgels of those clad in the pallium. For there will be no great difficulty in requesting, so to speak, the Herculean aid of the Cynics against the common plague. But if it should please me to contend with them for the sake of vain renown, a favor which should be granted me more readily since I am now applying myself to philosophy but I am not as yet a wise man, what will they have which they can refute? For behold! Let us suppose that the Academician and I have been implicated in those disputes of the philosophers; let all of them, indeed, be present; let them briefly explain their opinions according to the circumstances. Let Carneades be asked what he thinks. He will say that he is in doubt. And so one by one they will prefer him to the others; therefore the decision will be unanimous, an exceedingly great renown. Who would not desire to imitate him? And so, if I am asked, I shall give the same reply; my praise shall equal his. The wise man, therefore, rejoices in that honor in which the foolish man is made equal to him. What if even without difficulty he surpasses him? Does his self-respect have no influence upon him? For I shall detain that Academician who is now departing from the trial; perhaps in his folly he is rather eager for a victory of this kind. Therefore, after grasping hold of him, I shall make known to the judges what they do not know and I shall say: O eminent men, I have this in common with that man, the fact that he is in doubt as to who of you is striving after truth. But we also have our own opinions in regard to which I am asking you to pass judgment. For although I have heard your doctrines, I am uncertain where truth is, but it is for this reason that I do not know who among you is wise. That (Academician), however, denies that even the wise man himself knows anything, even wisdom itself whence he is said to be wise. Who would not see to whom the victory belongs? For if my opponent should say this, I shall excel him in renown; if, however, blushing with shame he will admit that the wise man knows wisdom, I shall be victorious over him by my opinion.

IX.   18. But let us withdraw from this now contentious tribunal to another place where there may be no disturbance to trouble us; would that it might be to the Academy of Plato which is said to have received its name from the fact that it was apart from the crowd.[22] Here let us discuss, in so far as we can, a subject not pertaining to renown, which is trivial and childish, but one relating to life itself and, in some way, to the hope of a happy soul. The Academicians say that nothing can be known. On what ground do you hold this opinion, O most zealous and learned men? They say: 'The definition of Zeno prompts us to formulate such an opinion.' But why, I ask you? For if that definition is true, he who knows it knows something true; if it is false, it should not have influenced men of great strength of character. But let us see what Zeno says: 'That, indeed, seems to be

---

[22] Cf. Diogenes Laertius, *Lives of Eminent Philosophers,* III, 7.

able to be grasped and apprehended which is of such a nature that it has no notes in common with what is false.'[23] Has this influenced you, O Platonist, to make every effort to deter from the hope of learning, those who are eager to do so, in order that they may altogether cease applying themselves to philosophy, since a certain deplorable inertness of mind is also of service to your endeavor?

19. But how would it fail to influence him if no such thing can be found and if, unless it is of such a character, it cannot be apprehended? If this is so, it should be said that wisdom cannot fall to the lot of man rather than that the wise man does not know why he is living, how he should live, whether he is living;[24] and finally nothing more perverse, nothing more foolish and absurd can be uttered than that a man is wise and that, at the same time, he does not know wisdom: For what is more unacceptable: that man cannot be wise, or that the wise man does not know wisdom? Hence there should be no argument if the case itself thus portrayed is not adequate for making a distinction between them. But if perchance, that were said, men would be thoroughly dissuaded from applying themselves to philosophy; now, indeed, they should be induced by the most delightful and sacred name of wisdom, when they have learned nothing after their life has been wasted, to pursue you afterwards with the loudest curses—you whom they have followed after abandoning, at least, the pleasures of the body for torments of mind.

20. But let us see by whom men are more greatly discouraged from the study of philosophy. Is it by him who says: 'Listen, my friend; philosophy is not called wisdom itself but the love of wisdom. If you devote yourself to it, you will not, indeed, be wise while you are living here in this world—for wisdom is found only with God and cannot be attained by man —but when you have applied yourself to it with sufficient diligence and have purified yourself, your soul will certainly enjoy wisdom after this life, that is, when you will have ceased to be mortal.' Or will you be deterred from the study of philosophy by him who says: 'Come, O mortals, to philosophy. Great is this reward; for what is dearer to man than wisdom? Come, therefore, in order that you may be wise and may not know wisdom!' 'I shall not speak in this manner,' he says. This is deceiving people; for nothing else will be found with you. The result is that, if you say this, they will flee from you as if you were insane; if you lead them to this opinion in any other way, you will make them insane. But, for the sake of both opinions, let us suppose that men do not want to apply themselves to philos-

---

[23] Cicero explains this doctrine of Zeno in *Academica*, II, xxiii, 77.
[24] Professor Gilson sees in this statement the first expression of what later on developed into the *Cogito*. Cf. E. Gilson, *Introduction a l'étude de saint Augustin* (Paris: J. Vrin, 1929), p. 46, n. 3.

ophy. If Zeno's definition demanded that something be said disadvantageous to philosophy, my dear man, should a person have been told that from which he would suffer grief or that on account of which he would scoff at you?

21. And yet, let us examine Zeno's definition in so far as we foolish men are able. It seemed to me, he said, that that could be apprehended which presented itself in such a way that it could not appear as false.[25] It is evident that nothing else comes into (the realm of) apprehension. I see this, said Arcesilaus, and for that very reason I teach that nothing is apprehended. For no such thing can be discovered. Perhaps it cannot by you and by other foolish men; but why can it not (be discovered) by a wise man? And yet I think that no reply can be given to the foolish man himself, if he should tell you to refute that very definition of Zeno by means of your remarkable keenness of intellect and to show that it can even be false. If you cannot do this, you have this very definition which you may apprehend; but if you disprove it, you do not have (a reason) by which you are prevented from apprehending. I do not see that it can be refuted and I consider it absolutely true. Therefore, when I know it, even though I may be foolish, I know something. But suppose this definition yields to your craftiness, I shall use a very safe disjunctive proposition. For either it is true or it is false. If it is true, I am right in holding fast to it; if it is false, something can be apprehended even if it has notes in common with what is false. Whence can this be? he says. Very correctly, therefore, has Zeno defined it nor has anyone who agreed with him on this point made an error. Or shall we consider the definition of little worth and clearness, which has proved itself such in opposition to those who intended to say a great deal against the ability of the mind to apprehend, since it pointed out what the nature was of that which could be apprehended? So in the case of matters to be apprehended, it is both a definition and an illustration. I do not know, he says, whether even the definition itself is true but, because it is probable, for that reason I maintain, in accord with it, that there is no such thing as it has represented (capable of) being apprehended. Perhaps you are going beyond the definition and you see, I believe, what follows as a logical consequence. But even if we are uncertain in regard to it, knowledge does not abandon us in this manner. For we know that it is either true or false; we do not therefore know nothing. Although it will never make me ungrateful, I certainly consider that definition very true. For either what is false can be known, which the Academicians greatly fear and which is truly absurd, or those things cannot be known which are very similar to what is false; therefore, that definition is true. And now let us investigate other matters.

---

[25] Cf. Cicero, *Academica*, II, xi, 34; II, xxxv, 112.

22. Although these arguments, if I am not mistaken, can be sufficient to insure a victory, perhaps they are not sufficient for a complete victory. There are two statements made by the Academicians which we started out to oppose in so far as we are able: that nothing can be apprehended, and that assent should not be given to anything.[26] We shall speak presently in regard to giving one's assent. For the time being, we shall say a few words more about apprehension. Do you say that absolutely nothing can be apprehended? At this point Carneades has awakened—for not one of the Academicians has slept less soundly than he—and he has carefully considered the intelligibility of things. So I suppose he soliloquizes somewhat as follows: Carneades, do you then intend to say that you do not know whether you are a man or an ant? Or will Chrysippus gain a victory over you? Let us say that we do not know those things that are sought for among philosophers, that other things do not concern us so that, if I err in the ordinary light of day, I may appeal to that darkness of the ignorant where only some divine eyes can see, which, even if they should behold me trembling and on the verge of falling, cannot reveal anything to the intellectually blind, especially to the proud and those who are ashamed to be taught anything. Indeed, O Greek diligence, you are progressing admirably well armed and equipped, but you are not considering that that definition is the invention of a philosopher and has been devised and firmly fixed at the entrance of philosophy. If you try to tear it down, it will get back on its feet again with double force. For though it has been weakened, not only can something be apprehended, but even that which closely resembles what is false can be apprehended, if you will not venture to destroy this definition. For it is your hiding place whence you violently rush forth and leap upon the unwary who desire to pass by; some Heroules[27] will strangle you in your cave as though you were half man and half animal and will overwhelm you by the difficulties of this same definition, teaching you that there is something in philosophy, which, although it is like what is false, you cannot make doubtful. But really I was hurrying on to other points. Whoever follows this up carefully, will insult you grievously, Carneades, since he thinks that I have left you dead at any place, or that you can be vanquished at any point. But if he does not think this, he is unmerciful since he forces me to abandon my post in a disorderly fashion and to contend with you in open warfare; when I began to come down upon you, I retreated, frightened by your name alone and I hurled down something from the higher place, which they saw under whose investigation we are now fighting, whether it reached you or whatever else became of it. But why should I be so foolish as to fear? If I remember correctly, you are dead and Alypius is no longer

---

[26] Cf. Cicero, *Academica*, II, xviii, 59.
[27] Cf. Vergil, *Aeneidos*, VIII, 194 ff.

before your tomb, fighting for your rights.[28] God will readily aid me against your shade.

23. You say that nothing can be apprehended in philosophy and, in order to spread your opinion far and wide, you make use of the disputes and contentions of philosophers and you think that these dissensions furnish arms for you against them. For how shall we determine the strife between Democritus[29] and the earlier natural philosophers about one world and innumerable worlds when no harmony could subsist between him and Epicurus, his successor? For when that lover of pleasure does not allow his atoms, his little maidservants, so to speak, that is, the little bodies which he joyfully embraces in the darkness, to hold their course, but permits them of their own accord to deviate here and there into strange by-paths, he has squandered his entire patrimony through contentions.[30] But this is of no concern to me. For if it belongs to wisdom to know any of these things, it cannot be hidden from the wise man. If, however, it is something else, the wise man knows that type of wisdom and despises such things as these. And yet, I who am still far removed from the likeness of a wise man, know something about those physical phenomena. For I hold as certain either that there is or is not one world; and if there is not one, there are either a finite or an infinite number of worlds.[31] Carneades would teach that that opinion resembles what is false. I likewise know that this world of ours has been so arranged either because of the nature of bodies or by some providence, and that it either always was and will be or that it began to exist and[32] will by no means cease existing, or that it does not have its origin in time but will have an end, or that it has started to remain in existence and will remain but not forever,[33] and I know innumerable physical phenomena of this type. For those disjunctions are true nor can anyone confuse them with any likeness to what is false. But take something for granted, says the Academician. I do not wish to do so; for that is to say: abandon what you know; say what you do not know. But opinion is uncertain. Assuredly it is better that it be uncertain than that it be destroyed; it surely is clear; it certainly now can be called false or true. I say that I know this opinion. Prove to me that I do not know them, you who do not

---

[28] At the close of the previous discussion, *Contra Academicos,* II, xiii, 30, Alypius had expressed approval of the doctrine of the Academicians, that certitude is impossible of attainment.

[29] Cf. Cicero, *Academica,* II, xl, 125.

[30] Cf. Cicero, *De finibus bonorum et malorum,* I, 18 ff; *De natura deorum,* I, 69; *De fato,* 21 ff.

[31] Augustine combats the skepticism of the New Academy by showing that certitude in regard to first and fundamental truths is furnished by the principle of contradiction.

[32] The variant *et minime* (codex Monacensis n. 14330; codex Trecensis n. 1085, editio Maurinorum) seems preferable to *minime,* found in the *Corpus scriptorum ecclesiasticorum Latinorum.*

[33] Cf. Cicero, *De natura deorum,* I, 20.

deny that such matters pertain to philosophy and who maintain that none of these things can be known; say that those disjunctive ideas are either false or have something in common with what is false from which they cannot altogether be distinguished.

XI. 24. Whence, he says, do you know that this world exists if the senses are untrustworthy? Your methods of reasoning have never been able to disprove the power of the senses in such a way as to convince us that nothing is seen and you certainly have never dared to try such a thing, but you have exerted yourself to persuade us urgently that (a thing) can be otherwise than it seems. And so I call this entire thing, whatever it is, which surrounds us and nourishes us, this object, I say, which appears before my eyes and which I perceive is made up of earth and sky, or what appears to be earth and sky, the world. If you say nothing is seen by me, I shall never err. For he is in error who rashly proves what seems to him. For you say that what is false can be seen by those perceiving it; you do not say that nothing is seen. Certainly every reason for arguing will be removed when it pleases you to settle the point, if we not only know nothing but if nothing is even seen by us. If, however, you deny that this object which appears to me is the world, you are making it a controversy in regard to a name since I said that I called it the world.

25. If you are asleep, you will say, is that also the world, which you see? I have already said I call that the world, which appears to me to be such. But if it pleases me to call only that the world, which is seen by those who are awake or even by those who are rational, prove this if you can, that those who are asleep and are raving are not raving and sleeping in the world.[34] Therefore I say this: that entire mass of bodies and that contrivance in which we exist whether sleeping, or raging, or awake, or rational, either is one or is not one. Explain how that opinion can be false. For if I am asleep, it can follow that I said nothing; or even if the words have escaped from the mouth of a person who is asleep, as often happens, it can follow that I did not speak here, nor while sitting in this way, nor to those who were listening; but it cannot follow that this is false. Nor do I say that I apprehended this because I am awake. For you can say that this could appear to me even if I were asleep and therefore this can bear a close resemblance to what is false. But if there are one and six worlds, it is evident to me, no matter in what condition I may be, that there are seven worlds, and I am not rash in asserting that I know it. Therefore, show me either that this logical conclusion or those disjunctions mentioned above in regard to sleep or madness or unreliability of the senses can be false, and I shall grant that I have been defeated if I remember them when I have been awakened. For I believe it is sufficiently evident that those things

---

[34] Cf. Cicero, *Academica*, II, xv, 48.

which appear false through sleep and an abnormal condition of the mind are those things which have reference to the senses of the body; for that three threes are nine and represent the square of intelligible numbers is necessary or would be true even though the human race were lying prostrate.[35] And yet I also see that many things can be said in favor of the senses themselves, which we have not found refuted by the Academicians. For I think that the senses are not to be blamed because they permit false and frenzied mental images or because in sleep we see things which are not true. If indeed the senses have reported the truth to those who are awake and who are rational, what the mind of a sleeping or insane person may fabricate for itself is not to be attributed to them.[36]

26. It now remains for us to inquire whether the senses report the truth when they give information.[37] Suppose that some Epicurean should say: 'I have no complaint to make in regard to the senses; for it is unjust to demand more of them than they can give; moreover whatever the eyes can see they see in a reliable manner.' Then is what they see in regard to an oar in the water true? It certainly is true. For when the reason is added for its appearing thus, if the oar dipped in the water seemed straight, I should rather blame my eyes for the false report. For they did not see what should have been seen when such causes arose. What need is there of many illustrations? This can also be said of the movement of towers, of the feathers of birds, of innumerable other things.[38] 'And yet I am deceived if I give my assent,' someone says. Do not give assent any further than to the extent that you can persuade yourself that it appears true to you, and there is no deception. For I do not see how the Academician can refute him who says: 'I know that this appears white to me, I know that my hearing is delighted with this, I know that this has an agreeable odor, I know that this tastes sweet to me, I know that this feels cold to me.' Tell us rather whether the leaves of the wild olive trees, which the goat so persistently desires, are by their very nature bitter. O foolish man! Is not the goat more reasonable? I do not know how they seem to the goat, but they are bitter to me. What more do you ask for? But perhaps there is also some one to whom they do not taste bitter. Do you trouble yourself about this? Did I say they were

---

[35] According to Augustine the unchanging character of mathematical truths is a cogent argument in favor of the certitude of knowledge.

[36] A somewhat similar line of argument is proposed by Descartes in his effort to discover a first and indubitable certitude. Cf. Descartes, *Meditations*, II, in *Meditations and Selections from the Principles of Philosophy*, translated by J. Veitch (Chicago; Open Court Publishing Co., 1931), p. 35.

[37] Cicero, *Academica*, II, xii, ff. and II, xxv, ff., discusses the validity of sense knowledge.

[38] Cicero also uses the illustrations of the bent oar and the changing colors of birds' feathers, as apparent deceptions of sense. Cf. *Academica*, II, vii, 19; II, xxv, 79. According to Diogenes Laertius, *Lives of Eminent Philosophers*, VII, 4, Zeno wrote a special work in which he treats of a large number of such deceptions.

bitter to everyone? I said they were bitter to me and I do not always maintain this. For what if for some reason or other a thing which now tastes sweet to a person should at another time seem bitter to him? I say this that, when a person tastes something, he can honestly swear that he knows it is sweet to his palate or the contrary, and that no trickery of the Greeks can dispossess him of that knowledge.[39] For who would be so bold as to say to me when I am longing for something with great pleasure: Perhaps you do not taste it, but this is only a dream? Do I offer any opposition to him? But still that would give me pleasure even in my sleep. Therefore no likeness to what is false obscures that which I have said I know, and both the Epicurean and the Cyrenaics[40] may say many other things in favor of the senses against which I have heard that the Academicians have not said anything. But why should this concern me? If they so desire and if they can, let them even do away with the argument with my approbation. Whatever argument they raise against the senses has no weight against all philosophers. For there are those who admit that whatever the mind receives through a sense of the body, can beget opinion, but they deny (that it can beget) knowledge which, however, they wish to be confined to the intellect and to live in the mind, far removed from the senses. And perhaps that wise man whom we are seeking is in their number.[41] But we shall say more about this at another time. Now let us proceed to those other points which, unless I am mistaken, we shall explain in a few words because of what has already been said.

XII.   27.   For how does any sense of the body help or hinder him who is inquiring into his moral life? Indeed, except in the case of those who have placed the highest and only true good of man in pleasure, neither the neck of a dove, nor a stammering voice,[42] nor a weight which is heavy for man but light for camels, nor six hundred other things prevent men from saying that they know they derive pleasure from that which affords them pleasure and that they are displeased by that which displeases them—a fact which I do not see can be refuted. Will such things disturb him whose

---

[39] Augustine here appeals to psychology in order to furnish evidence for the validity of our knowledge. Conscious experience when analyzed becomes a solid basis for certitude. Cf. *De beata vita*, II, ii, 7; *Soliloquia*, II, i, 1; *De libero arbitrio*, II, iii, 7; *De vera religione*, XL, lxxiii. In this respect we find Augustine in advance of Descartes and other modern philosophers.

[40] The Cyrenaics in their system of philosophy, developed tenets which were identical with those of the Epicureans. Hence Augustine mentions them together because of their agreement on the important rôle played by the senses in the attainment of knowledge as well as pleasure.

[41] While Augustine does not depreciate the importance of the senses for the acquisition of knowledge, he is convinced that the knowledge which makes for wisdom 'is confined to the intellect and lives in the mind, far removed from the senses.' The 'philosophers' whom Augustine mentions, in all probability, are the Platonists in whose estimation there is an essential difference between intellectual and sense knowledge.

[42] Cf. Cicero, *Academica,* II, vii, 19; II, xxv, 79.

mind is attached to the highest good? Which of these do you choose? If you ask me my opinion, I think that the highest good of man lies in his mind.[43] But now we are inquiring about knowledge. Then, ask the wise man who cannot be ignorant of wisdom; however, it is even permitted me who am stupid and foolish, to know that the highest good of man in which a happy life consists, is either nothing, or it is found in the soul, or in the body, or in both together. Prove, if you can, that I do not know this, since those well known reasons of yours in no way do so. If you cannot—for you will not find that it has any resemblance to what is false—shall I rightly hesitate to conclude that it seems to me the wise man knows whatever is true in philosophy since I have learned so many truths from that source?

28. But perhaps he is afraid that he may choose the highest good while sleeping. 'There is no danger;'[44] when he wakes up, he will reject it, if it is displeasing to him; if he likes it, he will hold fast to it. For who will rightly blame him because in his sleep he has seen something that is not true? Or will you fear, perhaps, that while sleeping he may lose wisdom if he approves of what is false instead of true? Indeed, not even would a sleeping man foolishly dare to imagine that he should call a man wise when he is awake and deny that he is so if he is asleep. This can likewise be said about frenzy. But my discourse is hastening on to other points. Still, I shall not leave this topic without drawing a very safe conclusion. For either wisdom is lost in a state of frenzy and he will no longer be wise whom you are proclaiming to be ignorant of truth, or his knowledge remains in his intellect even if the other part of his mind imagines, just as in sleep, what it has received from the senses.

XIII. 29. There now remains dialectic which the wise man certainly knows well, and no one can know what is false. If, indeed, he does not know it, the knowledge of that without which he could be wise does not belong to wisdom and it is needless for us to inquire whether it is true or whether it can be apprehended. At this point perhaps someone may say to me: 'Are you, foolish man, accustomed to relate what you know or were you unable to know anything about dialectic?' Indeed I know more about it than about any other part of philosophy. For in the first place, it has taught me that all those propositions which I have previously made use of are true. Moreover, I have learned through dialectic that many other things

---

[43] In *Retractationes*, I, i, 9, Augustine remarks that it would be more correct to say that the highest good of man is found in God: 'Verius dixissem: in Deo; ipso enim mens fruitur, ut beata sit, tamquam bono summo suo.'
[44] Terence, *Andreos*, 350; *Phormio*, 763.

are true.[45] Count, if you can, how many there are: if there are four elements in the world, there are not five; if there is one sun, there are not two; one and the same soul cannot die and still be immortal; man cannot at the same time be happy and unhappy; if the sun is shining here, it cannot be night; we are now either awake or asleep; either there is a body which I seem to see or there is not a body. Through dialectic I have learned that these and many other things which it would take too long to mention are true; no matter in what condition our senses may be, these things are true of themselves. It has taught me that, if the antecedent of any of those statements which I just placed before you in logical connection were assumed, it would be necessary to deduce that which was connected with it; in fact, that those things which were predicated by me as contraries or as disjunctives have this nature, that, when the other parts, whether they be one or more, are taken away, something remains which is established by their removal. It has likewise taught me that, when certainty is established in regard to any matter that is being discussed, there should be no further argument on that point, and that whoever does so should be instructed if he does it through ignorance, and should be ignored if he does it through malice; if he cannot be taught, he should be advised to do something else rather than waste his time and his energy on what is not necessary, and if he does not comply, no attention should be paid to him. But in regard to sophistries and fallacious syllogisms, this brief rule has been laid down: if they are caused by a wrong concession, one ought to abandon what has been conceded; but if a true and a false statement are involved in one conclusion, what is known should be accepted, what cannot be explained should be rejected; if, however, a proper measure (modus) in regard to some matters is entirely concealed from man, the knowledge of it ought not be sought. Indeed from dialectic I have learned all these points and many others which it is not necessary to mention, for I ought not appear ungrateful. Truly that wise man either overlooks these facts, or if dialectic when acquired is itself the knowledge of truth, he knows it in such a way that he destroys by ignoring and not taking pity on its hunger that very flimsy trick of theirs: if a thing is true, it is false; if it is false, it is true. I think nothing more need be said about apprehension since the whole matter will be treated again when I begin to speak about giving assent.

XIV. 30. Now, then, let us come to that part in regard to which Alypius still seems to be in doubt, and first of all let us examine that, whatever it may be, which renders you most shrewd and circumspect. For if this discovery of yours, by which we are forced to admit that it is much

---

[45] Augustine holds that the certitude provided by the fundamentals of dialectic is a strong argument in refutation of the skepticism of the New Academy. In the *De ordine,* in which he is loud in his praise of dialectic, he calls it 'the discipline of disciplines.' Cf. *De ordine,* II, xiii, 38.

more probable that the wise man knows wisdom, weakens the opinion of the Academicians, strengthened as it was—this was your statement—by so many and such valid reasons, according to which they believed that the wise man knows nothing, assent ought all the more be withheld. For by this very point it is proved that he cannot be persuaded even by the most abundant and subtle arguments, who is not opposed by a contrary faction, if it has the ability to do so, with no less bitterness or even more. From this it follows that, although the Academician has been vanquished, he has been victorious. Would that he were vanquished! He will never succeed by any kind of Greek strategy in departing from me vanquished and, at the same time, victorious.[46] Certainly if nothing else may be found to be brought against those arguments, I shall acknowledge of my own accord that I have been vanquished. For we are not concerned with the attaining of renown, but with the finding of truth. It is sufficient for my purpose to get past, in any way whatsoever, that boulder which stands in the way of those entering philosophy[47] and which, while concealing the darkness in some kind of receptacles, boastfully asserts that the whole of philosophy is such and does not permit one to hope that any light will be found in it. But I have nothing more to desire if it is now probable that the wise man knows something. For it did not seem probable for any other reason that he ought to withhold his assent except for the fact that it was probable that nothing can be apprehended. Since this has been removed—for the wise man actually apprehends wisdom itself, as is now granted—no further reason will remain for the wise man's not assenting to wisdom itself. For, without doubt, it is more unheard of for the wise man not to approve of wisdom than it is for him not to know wisdom.

31. For let us picture to ourselves for a little while, I ask you, such a spectacle as a kind of dispute between a wise man and wisdom. What else does wisdom say than that she herself is wisdom? But he, on the other hand, says: 'I do not believe it.' Who is it that says to wisdom: 'I do not believe that there is such a thing as wisdom'?[48] Who, indeed, except that wise man with whom wisdom was able to speak and in whom she deigned to dwell? Come now and inquire of me who am fighting with the Acade-

---

[46] Cf. Vergil, *Aeneidos*, II, 152.

[47] Augustine considers it of the utmost importance to prove that truth is accessible to man. This he regards as the foundation upon which the structure of philosophy is erected. In the *De beata vita* which was written between the first and second books of the *Contra Academicos* he also calls attention to 'an enormous mountain situated before the harbor of philosophy.' Cf. *De beata vita*, I, i, 3. This obstacle to the attainment of wisdom, he remarks, is pride which is synonymous with error and therefore an impediment to truth which leads to wisdom.

[48] At this point in his criticism of the Academicians, *Contra Academicos*, III, xiv, 31-32, Augustine takes pains to show the absurdity of applying the term *sapiens* to man if, as the Academicians hold, truth is unattainable, and consequently if man to whom the appellation *sapiens* is given can not know that there is such a thing as wisdom.

micians; now you have a new contest: a wise man and wisdom are fighting with each other. The wise man does not wish to assent to wisdom. I am safe in waiting with you (for the outcome). For who would not believe that wisdom is inconquerable? And yet, let us be prepared for some kind of a dilemma. For in this contest either the Academician will vanquish wisdom and will be conquered by me because he will not be wise, or he will be defeated by wisdom and we shall prove that the wise man assents to wisdom. Therefore, either the Academician is not wise or the wise man will assent to something, unless perhaps he who was ashamed to say that the wise man does not know wisdom, will not be ashamed to say that the wise man does not assent to wisdom. But if it is now probable that this will befall the wise man or the apprehension of wisdom itself, and if there is no reason why he should not give assent to what can be apprehended, I see what I desired should be probable—that the wise man will surely assent to wisdom. If you ask me where he will find wisdom itself, I shall reply: 'In himself.'[49] If you say that he does not know what he possesses, you are returning to that absurd statement that the wise man does not know wisdom. If you say that the wise man himself cannot be found, we shall no longer discuss this subject with the Academicians, but we shall treat of it in another conversation with you, whoever you are, that have this notion. For when they argue this point, they are arguing, indeed, about the wise man. Cicero asserts[50] that he himself is a great conjecturer but that he is inquiring about the wise man. If you are not yet familiar with this, my young friends, you certainly have read it in the *Hortensius*: 'If, then, nothing at all is certain and if it is not the part of a wise man to form an opinion, the wise man will never assent to anything.'[51] From this it is evident that they are inquiring about the wise man in those very arguments of theirs against which we are contending.

32.   And so I think that the wise man certainly possesses wisdom, that is, that the wise man has apprehended wisdom and for this reason he is not conjecturing when he assents to wisdom; for he is giving assent to that without the apprehension of which he would not be wise. Those (Academicians) do not assert that a person ought not give assent, except in regard to those things which cannot be apprehended; but wisdom is not nothing: therefore, when he both knows wisdom and assents to wisdom, the wise man neither knows nothing nor does he give assent to nothing. What more do you desire? Are we inquiring about that error which they say is entirely avoided if the mind refrains from giving assent to anything? For he is in

[49] That truth in its perfection is discovered within the human mind is a doctrine emphasized by Augustine in his early treatises. Cf. *De magistro*, XI, 38; XII, 40; *De vera religione*, CXXX, 55; *Epistulae*, XIX, 1.
[50] Cf. Cicero, *Academica*, II, xxi, 66.
[51] Cicero, *Hortensius*, fragment 100.

error, they say, who assents not only to what is false but also to what is doubtful, even though it may be true. But I find nothing which may not be doubtful. Yet at least the wise man finds wisdom itself, as we said.

XV. 33. But perhaps you now wish me to dismiss this (argument). What is very certain ought not readily be abandoned. We are dealing with very clever men; and yet I shall comply with your wishes. But what am I to say at this point? What indeed? Undoubtedly that old statement ought to be made when they themselves have something to say. For what am I to do since you are forcing me out of my own camp? Shall I implore the aid of the more learned, since perhaps I shall be less ashamed to be vanquished if I cannot conquer with their help? And so I shall hurl with all the strength at my disposal a weapon smoky indeed and mean but, if I am not mistaken, a very powerful one; he who gives assent to nothing, does nothing. O unsophisticated man! And where is probability? Where is the likeness of truth? You desired this. Do you hear how the Greek shields are resounding? The strongest weapon has been taken up but with what skill have we hurled it! Those opponents of mine furnish me with no more powerful weapon and I have not inflicted a wound, so far as I see. I shall direct my attention to what my villa and the open country provide; greater things are a burden rather than a help to me.

34. When I had reflected long and leisurely in that atmosphere of the country how this same probability or likeness of truth can protect our deeds from error, at first it seemed to me, as usually happened when I devoted myself to such considerations, that it was intricately obscure and well guarded; then when I looked at the entire problem more carefully, it seemed to me that I saw one entrance by which error might rush upon those who are certain. For I think that not only he is in error who follows the wrong path, but also he who does not follow the right one. Let us take the case of two travelers going toward one and the same place. One of them has determined not to believe anyone and the other is too credulous. They have arrived at a certain place where two roads meet. Hereupon the credulous man says to a shepherd who happened to be there, or to some peasant: 'Hail, my good man! Tell me, I beg of you, the road which best leads to that place.' The peasant replies: 'If you take this road, you will not make a mistake.' And the former says to his companion: 'He is telling the truth; let us go by this road.' His very cautious companion laughs at and wittily makes sport of him who has given his assent so quickly and in the meantime, while the latter is departing, the prudent man stands rooted to the place where the two roads meet. And now he begins to feel ashamed for hesitating, when behold! from another corner of the road a certain refined and distinguished looking man appears riding on his horse and begins to come toward him. The traveler rejoices and, after greeting the man

[74]

who is approaching him, he makes known his difficulty, inquires about the road, and even tells him the reasons for his remaining there in order to render his informant more favorably disposed to him by preferring him to the shepherd. But by chance he was evidently one of those who now are ordinarily called buffoons [samardocos]. The wicked man even of his own accord observed his usual line of conduct. 'Take this road,' he says, 'for I am coming from that direction.' So he deceived him and went along his way. But when should that (traveler of ours) be deceived? For I do not give assent to that direction as if it were true, he says, but because it is probable and because it is neither right nor advantageous to loiter here; so I should go by this road. Meanwhile, he who erred by giving his assent so quickly in believing that the words of the shepherd were true, was already relaxing in that place which he set out to reach; his companion, however, not being in error if he followed what seemed probable, roamed around forests of various kinds and still did not find anyone who knew the place to which he had intended to go. To tell the truth, when I thought about that illustration, I could not refrain from laughing, since somehow it follows from the words of the Academicians that he is in error who holds the right road by chance but that he does not seem to err who probably was led through mountains far out of his way and did not attain his desired goal. For rightly to condemn giving one's assent rashly, it is more likely that both are in error rather than that the latter does not err. Hence, in opposition to those words of theirs, I began to be more observant in reflecting on the deeds and conduct of men. Then, indeed, so many and such strong arguments against them occurred to me that I no longer laughed at them but I became, to some extent, irritated and, to some extent, sorry that very learned and keen minded men had become involved in such disgraceful offenses as reducing certitude to mere opinion.

XVI. 35. For it is certain that perhaps not everyone who errs is guilty of sin, but still it is granted that he who sins either is guilty of error or of something worse. What if some youth, then, when he hears these men saying: 'It is disgraceful to err and for that reason we ought not assent to anything; but yet, when each one does what seems probable to him, he neither hesitates nor errs, but merely remembers that whatever occurred to his mind or to his senses should not be assented to as if it were true'—upon hearing this, then, will the young man plot against the chastity of another man's wife? I am asking you, Marcus Tullius, for your advice; we are considering the moral lives of young men and all your letters provided for the training and guidance of their lives. What else will you say but that in your opinion it is not probable that the youth would do this? But it seems probable to him. For if we live on another's probability, you would not have guided the destiny of the state because it seemed to Epicurus that you ought not have done so. And so that youth will commit adultery with another man's wife; if he is caught at it, where will he find you to defend him? And yet, even if he should find you, what will you have to say? No doubt, you will deny it. What if it is so clear that it is futile for you to deny it? Undoubtedly you wish to persuade him, just as in the gymnasium of Cumae and even that of Naples, that he did not sin, nay more, that he did not even err. For he persuaded himself that as a matter of fact adultery ought not be committed; it occurred to him as probable, he yielded, he committed it; or perhaps he did not commit it but it seemed to him that he did so. But that woman's husband, foolish man, makes a great disturbance, defending his wife's virtue in the courts when perhaps he is now sleeping with her and does not know it. If those judges find this out, either they will disregard the Academicians and punish this as being a genuine crime or, if they agree with these same Academicians, it is very likely and probable that they will declare the man guilty, with the result that the defender is wholly at a loss to know what to do. He will not have a chance to become angry with anyone since they all say that they did not err inasmuch as they did what seemed probable, while not giving their assent. And so he will lay aside the rôle of defender and assume the consoling character of a philosopher; thus he will readily persuade the youth who has already made such progress in the Academy, to think, just as if he were asleep, that he was declared guilty. But you think that I am joking. I can swear by all that is divine[52] that I am utterly at a loss to know how he sinned, if whoever does what seems probable is not guilty of sin, unless perhaps they say that to err is one thing, while to sin is quite another, and that they intended by those precepts that we should not err, but that they thought that committing sin is of no great consequence.

36.   I make no mention at all of the murders, parricides, sacrileges, and all other excesses and crimes which can be committed or thought of, which are defended in few words and, what is more serious, even by very wise judges:[53] I have not assented to anything and therefore I have not erred; moreover, how should I not do what seemed probable? But those who do not think that through probability people can be persuaded to (commit) such deeds, should read the speech of Catiline[54] by which he won his country over to parricide, an act in which all crimes are contained. Now who does not laugh at this? They say that in their actions they are striving after nothing except probability and they are earnestly seeking truth although it seems likely to them that it cannot be found. O strange spectacle! But let

[52] Cf. Terence, *Eunichos,* 331. In *Retractationes,* I, i, 10-11, Augustine remarks: 'Nec illud mihi placet, quod dixi; *liquet deiurare per omne divinum.*'
[53] Augustine stresses (*Contra Academicos,* III, xvi, 35-36) the serious moral disorder to which skepticism leads and which is one of its most disastrous results.
[54] Cf. Sallust, *Catiline,* XX.

us pass over this point; it has less reference to us, to the danger threatening our life, to the peril of our fortunes. But this is of vast importance, this is appalling, this ought to be feared by every good man, namely, that he may commit every kind of sin not only without the blame of crime but even without the blame of error if this probable line of reasoning will be (followed)—when it seems to anyone that what is probable should be done, he should merely not assent to anything as if it were true.—What then? Did they not see this point? Yes indeed, they very cleverly and wisely saw it, nor should I in any way lay claim to tread in the steps of Marcus Tullius in any respect, in diligence, alertness, ability, learning; and yet if only this were said to him when he stated that man cannot know anything: 'I know that this seems so to me,' he would have no grounds on which to refute it.

XVII. 37. Why, then, have such great men desired to engage in such continuous and persistent controversies, that the knowledge of truth might not seem to fall to the lot of anyone? Now, listen rather carefully for a little while not to what I know, but to what I think about it.[55] I kept this point for the conclusion of my talk in order to explain, if I could, how the entire strategem of the Academicians appears to me. It is said that Plato, the wisest and most learned man of his age, who spoke in such a way that whatever he said became important and who so expressed himself that, in whatever manner he spoke, his words did not lose their importance,[56] also learned many things from the Pythagoreans after the death of his teacher, Socrates,[57] whom he had greatly loved. But Pythagoras, who was dissatisfied with Greek philosophy which at that time did not amount to much or, at least, was very obscure, after having believed that the soul is immortal, being influenced to that conviction by the arguments of a certain Syrian, Pherecydes,[58] had also heard many wise men as he traveled about far and wide. So Plato, by adding to the Socratic charm and subtlety which he had in his ethical teachings the knowledge of things human and divine which

---

[55] Augustine introduces his theory in regard to the esoteric doctrines of the Academicians tentatively and not as a matter of fact.

[56] In the writings of Augustine we find repeated expression of his deep affection and high regard for Plato, not only in the early treatises but in his later works as well. Cf. *Soliloquia*, I, iv, 9; *Epistulae*, I, 1; VII, i, 2; *De civitate Dei*, II, 8, 14; VIII, 5; VIII, 11; X, 30; XI, 25; XXII, 28.

In the *Retractationes*, II, xviii, 41, Augustine disapproves of the excessive praise bestowed upon the Platonic philosophers in the *Contra Academicos*: 'Laus quoque ipsa, qua Platonem vel Platonicos seu Academicos philosophos tantum extuli quantum impios homines non oportuit, non immerito mihi displicuit.'

[57] Augustine's familiarity with the writings of Plato probably acquainted him with the latter's deep affection for his teacher, Socrates. Cf. *Confessiones*, I, xvi, 25; I, xiii, 22; VIII, v, 11; VIII, vii, 18; X, x, 17; XIII, iv, 5.

[58] Cicero mentions that Pythagoras was the pupil of Pherecydes and that he accepted his teacher's doctrine of the immortality of the human soul. Cf. *Tusculanae disputationes*, I, xvi, 38: 'Pherecydes Syrius primum dixit animos esse hominum sempiternos antiquus sane; . . . hanc opinionem discipulus eius Pythagoras maxime confirmavit.'

he had carefully received from those whom I have mentioned, and by joining with them dialectic, the judge and organizer of these parts, so to speak, which either should be wisdom itself or without which there could be no wisdom at all, is said to have formulated a perfect system of philosophy, which it is not opportune at the present time to discuss. It is sufficient for my purpose that Plato thought that there were two worlds:[59] the one, intelligible where truth itself dwelt; the other, sensible, which, as is clear, we feel by sight and touch. And so (he thought) that the former was the true world; the latter, the likeness of the true world and fashioned to its image, and therefore from the former world truth could be refined, so to speak, and be made clear, as it were, in that soul which knew itself; from the latter, however, not knowledge but opinion could be generated in the souls of the foolish; and yet whatever was done in this world through those virtues which he called virtues befitting a citizen (civiles), like other true virtues which were unknown except to a few wise men, could be given no other name except the likeness of truth.

38. I am of the opinion that these and other teachings of this kind were kept by his successors in so far as they were able, and were carefully guarded as mysteries. For either they are not readily understood except by those who, while purifying themselves from all vices, have laid claim to a different mode of life higher than that on a merely human level, or he who, knowing these doctrines, has wished to teach all other men does not fall into serious error. And so I imagine that Zeno, the founder of the Stoics, was held in suspicion when, after hearing and believing some (of these teachings), he came into the school left by Plato, which Polemo[60] at that time was keeping up; nor did he seem to be the type of a man[61] to whom those doctrines of Plato, as something sacred, should readily be handed over and entrusted, before he had unlearned those teachings which he had received from others and had brought into that school. When Polemo died, Arcesilaus succeeded him, in reality a fellow-student of Zeno[62] but under the tutorship of Polemo. For this reason when Zeno was pleased with a certain opinion of his own in regard to the world and especially concerning the soul for which true philosophy is ever watchful, saying that

---

[59] Augustine seems to have known Plato exactly in regard to the latter's doctrine of the two worlds. Cf. *Phaedo*, 65a-68b; *Parmenides*, 126a-135c. The distinction between the intelligible and sensible worlds is also mentioned by Augustine in *Epistulae*, III, 1; IV, 2; *De magistro*, XII, 39-40.

[60] Diogenes Laertius, *Lives of Eminent Philosophers*, VII, 25, tells a story about Polemo accusing Zeno of stealing Academic doctrine.

[61] In *Tusculanae disputationes*, V, 34, Cicero calls Zeno 'ignobilis verborum opifex.'

[62] The jealousy between Arcesilaus and Zeno, both students of Polemo, is usually regarded as the reason for the foundation of the Stoic and New Academic Schools. Cf. Cicero, *Academica*, II, ix, 35. Diogenes Laertius, *Lives of Eminent Philosophers*, VII, 1, mentions Polemo among the teachers of Zeno; however, among the masters of Arcesilaus he does not mention Polemo.

it is perishable and that there is nothing beyond this sensible world and it consists of nothing but matter[63]—for he thought that the deity itself is fire[64]—Arcesilaus, in my opinion, very wisely and profitably concealed the doctrine of the Academy, since that evil was spreading far and wide, and he buried the gold, so to speak, to be discovered at some future time by posterity. Therefore, since the ordinary run of people is somewhat inclined to rush into false conjectures, and since it is very readily but culpably believed that all things are material after the fashion of bodies, this very keen minded and cultured man began to unteach those whom he noticed were badly taught rather than to teach those whom he did not regard as capable of being taught. Hence all those doctrines originated which are ascribed to the New Academy because the older Academies did not have any need for them.[65]

39. But if Zeno at some time had been aroused and had observed that nothing can be known unless it were such as he himself defined, and that nothing such can be found in corporeal things to which he attributed everything, this kind of arguing which he had necessarily stirred up would some time have been entirely blotted out. But, according to the opinion of the Academicians themselves and in my opinion also, Zeno, deceived by the appearance of consistency, held firmly (to his doctrine) and that pernicious materialistic belief was preserved, in whatever way he found possible, by Chrysippus who, being a very able man, was making every effort to spread it further if Carneades, a more keen and vigilant man,[66] had not opposed other higher teachings of that school in such a way that I am surprised that this doctrine of theirs even afterwards attained any prominence. For, first of all, lest it should seem that he wished to oppose all their doctrines just to make an impression, Carneades put an end to the audacity, as it were, of their tricky attacks, by which he observed that Arcesilaus had, in no slight measure, been maligned, but he especially intended that those Stoics and Chrysippus should be overwhelmed and destroyed.

XVIII. 40. Then when he was assailed from all sides (with the objection) that the wise man would do nothing if he did not assent to anything[67]—O strange man and yet not so strange either! for he issued from the very fountains of Plato—he wisely directed his attention to such actions as they were wont to give assent to and, seeing that they bore some resemblance to what was true, he called that which a person should strive

---

[63] Cf. Diogenes Laertius, *Lives of Eminent Philosophers*, VII, 134.
[64] *Ibid..* VII, 136, 137.
[65] Cf. Cicero, *Academica*, I, xii, 43-46.
[66] Cicero speaks of Carneades as a man 'nullius philosophiae partis ignarus,' and 'incredibili quadam facultate.' Cf. *Academica*, I, xii, 46.
[67] Cf. Cicero, *Academica*, II, 39, 62, 108; *De finibus bonorum et malorum*, IV, xxv, 46. The skepticism of the New Academy, according to the dogmatists, cut away the ground, so to speak, from action and duty.

to attain in this world the likeness of truth.[68] For he was clever enough to know and wise enough to conceal that to which the likeness might be, and so he named it probability. He certainly is right in giving assent to the image, who beholds its archetype. For how does the wise man give assent to or how does he strive after the likeness of truth if he does not know what truth itself is? Therefore, they knew and assented to what is false[69] if they noticed in it a worthy imitation of truth. But because it was neither right nor easy to show this to the uninitiated, as it were, they left it to posterity and to those to whom at that time they were able to convey a certain idea of their meaning, but they rightly forbade those dialecticians to raise any question in regard to words, reviling and ridiculing them. For these reasons Carneades is also said to have been the founder and chief exponent of the Third Academy.

41. That conflict then continued even up to the time of our Cicero, though now it is evidently weak and about to exhale its last breath upon Latin literature. For, in my opinion, nothing is more insolent than that a person should speak very profusely and eloquently about something with which he himself does not agree. And yet it was by these winds, it seems to me, that the worthless doctrine of Antiochus[70] of the Platonic Academy was disseminated and spread abroad. For the herd of Epicureans erected their sunny stables in the minds of voluptuous people. Antiochus, forsooth, a disciple of Philo,[71] a very prudent man, I believe, who had already begun to open the gates, so to speak, to the enemy who were retiring and to call back the Academy and its doctrines to the authority of Plato—although Metrodorus[72] had previously attempted to do this, who is said to

---

[68] Cicero represents Clitomachus, the pupil of Carneades, as teaching this doctrine. Cf. *Academica,* II, x, 32.

[69] In *Retractationes,* I, i, 11, Augustine expresses disapproval of this mode of expression: 'Item quod dixi de Academicis, quia noverant verum, cuius ideam appellabant verisimile, idque ipsum verisimile appellavi falsum, quod adprobabant, duas ob causas non recte dictum est, vel quod falsum esset, quod aliquo modo esset simile alicuius veri, quia in genere suo et hoc verum est, vel quod adprobabant ista falsa, quae vocabant verisimilia, cum illi nihil adprobarent et adfirmarent nihil adprobare sapientem. Sed quia hoc ipsum verisimile etiam probabile nuncupabant, hinc factum est, ut de illis dicerem.'

[70] Cicero speaks of his teacher, Antiochus of Ascalon, with great praise. Cf. *Tusculanae disputationes,* III, xxv, 59; *Brutus,* 91, 315. Augustine probably characterizes him as *faeneus* because he attempted to show that the Stoic doctrines were really to be found in Plato. Cf. Cicero, *Academica,* II, 45, 137; *De finibus bonorum et malorum,* V, 3, 7.

[71] About 110 B.C. Philo succeeded Clitomachus as head of the New Academic School. However, toward the end of his life he ceased to preach the pure doctrine of Carneades, and when he died, the New Academy practically became extinct. Cf. *Academica,* II, iv, 11.

[72] Metrodorus of Stratonice is maintained by Cicero as an authority for the opinions of Carneades. Cf. *Academica,* II, vi, 16; I, fragment 35. He preceded Philo in his reaction against extreme skepticism and affirmed that Carneades had been misunderstood by all his hearers. Cf. also *De oratore,* 51. Augustine seems to

have been the first to admit that the doctrine, that nothing could be known, was not exactly to the liking of the Academicians but that they had been obliged to take up arms of this kind against the Stoics—and so Antiochus, as I had started to say, having listened to Philo, the Academician, and Muesarchus, the Stoic, against the Old Academy which was without defenders, and safe, as it were, since there was no enemy, had crept in as a helper and a citizen, bringing in some evil doctrine from the ashes of the Stoics to profane the shrines of Plato.[73] But Philo opposed him by again snatching away those arms until he died, and our Cicero destroyed every remnant of his doctrine, since, as long as he lived, he did not allow whatever he had loved, to be corrupted or contaminated. And so shortly after that time all their obstinacy and persistency died out and after the clouds of error had been dispelled, the countenance of Plato, which is the purest and the brightest in all philosophy, shone forth especially in the person of Plotinus,[74] a Platonic philosopher, who was considered so much like Plato that one would have to believe that they lived at the same time, but so great an interval elapsed between them that one would have to think that the latter had come to life again in the person of the former.

XIX. 42. And so we rarely see philosophers now except the Cynics, or the Peripatetics, or the Platonists, and especially the Cynics, since they take delight in a certain laxity and unrestraint in their manner of living. However, one school of the most genuine philosophy has expressed, I believe, what pertains to knowledge, doctrine, and code of morals which have regard for the interests of the soul, since very keen and clever men were not wanting who in their arguments taught that Aristotle and Plato agreed with them to such an extent that they seem to be different from the inexperienced and less enlightened during many ages and in many disputes.[75] For it is not the philosophy of this world, which our sacred writings very rightly abhor, but of another intelligible world to which the most subtle reasoning would never recall souls enveloped in the manifold darkness of error and defiled by the sordid appetites of the body, if the Omnipotent God in His mercy toward mankind did not abase and degrade the greatness of His divine Mind by assuming a human body in order that souls, en-

---

agree with Cicero in regarding Metrodorus as the first Academician teacher who openly taught that the skepticism of his predecessors was merely used as a defense measure. Cf. *Contra Academicos,* III, xvii, 38; III, xviii, 41.

[73] Cf. note 70.

[74] Augustine seems to have regarded Plotinus as a follower of Plato, and Neo-Platonism and Platonism as one and the same school of philosophy. Cf. *Epistulae,* VI, 1; *De civitate Dei,* VIII, 12; X, 2; IX, 10; X, 14.

[75] Augustine evidently is of the opinion that the real Academicians, the Platonists and the Peripatetics, adhered to one and the same body of doctrine. Cf. *De civitate Dei,* IX, 4. It would seem that Augustine accepted this notion from Cicero who expressed the opinion that the Academicians and Peripatetics, though differing in names, were of the same sect. Cf. *Tusculanae disputationes,* I, 18.

kindled not only by His words but also by His example,[76] might be able to return to themselves and without the wrangling of arguments to have a taste of their true country.

XX. 43. Meanwhile I have convinced myself, in so far as I was able, in regard to this probability of the Academicians. If it is false, it does not concern me since it is now sufficient for me not to believe that truth cannot be attained by man. But whoever is of the opinion that the Academicians thought this should listen to Cicero himself. For he says that they were accustomed to conceal their doctrine and to hide it from everyone except those who lived with them to the period of old age.[77] What their doctrine really is, however, (only) God will know; and yet I think it was that of Plato. But in order that you may briefly hear my unqualified statement as to what human wisdom is of itself, I admit that I have not apprehended (its nature). Yet, although I am now in my thirty-third year, I do not think I ought to despair of ever attaining wisdom. Having despised all other things which men consider good, I have set out to devote my efforts to search for it. Since the doctrines of the Academicians did not lightly deter me from this important business, I have been well fortified against their teachings, I believe, by this argument of yours. But no one doubts that we are incited to learn by the double weight of authority and of reason. Therefore I am sure that I shall never depart from the authority of Christ; for I find no other more reliable.[78] But what ought to be attained by the most subtle reasoning—for at the present time I am so disposed as impatiently to desire to apprehend truth not only by believing, but also by knowing— I trust I shall find meanwhile in the works of the Platonists,[79] what is not in contradiction with our sacred writings.'

44. At this point, after they saw that I had ended the discussion, although night had come on and part of our conversation had even been written by lamplight, still the young men were waiting with great eagerness to see whether Alypius would promise to make a reply to it on the following day. Then Alypius said: 'I am ready to assert that nothing ever

---

[76] In his early works Augustine seems to assign to the Incarnate God the special rôle of a Divine Teacher and Exemplar—an intellectual Guide, as it were, through whom man could arrive at a knowledge of truth. Cf. *Epistulae*, XI, 4.

[77] Cf. Cicero, *Academica*, I, fragment 21; II, xviii, 60. Augustine likewise seems to be of the opinion that the Academicians held as esoteric doctrines the teachings of Plato and that they made a pretense of skepticism in order to mislead those who were incapable of understanding their exalted views.

[78] At the very beginning of his conversion Augustine stresses that there are two sources of religious knowledge: reason and authority. This thesis is also developed in *De ordine*, II, ix, 26.

[79] At the time of the writing of this treatise Augustine was so deeply impressed by the spiritual element in Platonic philosophy, that he seemed convinced that from it he could derive assistance in understanding more clearly the mysteries of faith. In the *Retractationes*, I, i, 12 he expresses regret for this exaggerated confidence in the Platonists, adding that 'Christian doctrine ought to be defended against their grievous errors.'

turned out so contrary to my expectation as that I am departing from this argument today, vanquished. I do not think this happiness ought merely to be mine. Therefore, I shall share it with you, my rivals or our judges, since even the Academicians themselves perhaps desired to be vanquished in that way by their descendants. For what could be displayed or presented to us more pleasing than the charm of this discourse, what more worthy of consideration than the importance of its content, what more manifest than its beneficence, what more practical than its doctrine? Indeed, I find it impossible worthily to express my admiration that a bitter subject was treated so wittily; a hopeless topic, so resolutely; an argument proved conclusively, with such moderation; an obscure theme, so lucidly. For that reason, my companions, change your desire of challenging me to reply into that of learning with me with a more certain hope. We have a leader who can conduct us to the very secrets of truth, with God now pointing out the way.'

45.   When the young men with a kind of childish eagerness showed by the expression on their faces that they had been cheated, so to speak, because Alypius did not intend to make a reply to my argument, I said smilingly: 'Do you envy me the praise I have received? But since now I am sure of the support of Alypius and do not have to fear him, in order that you also may be grateful to me, I shall draw you up in line of battle against him who has foiled your expectation. Read the *Academica* and when you have there found Cicero the victor over that nonsense—for what will be easier—compel Alypius to defend this discussion of ours against those unanswerable objections. I assign you this difficult task, Alypius, to repay you for the praise you bestowed upon me, of which I was undeserving.' At this point they all laughed and we brought this great argument to a close— whether permanently or not, I do not know—but, at all events, more calmly and quickly than I had hoped for.

INDEX